ISLAMIC
NAMES

ISLAMIC
NAMES

by
M. Imran Ashraf Usmani

Islamic Book Service

ISLAMIC NAMES
By M. Imran Ashrsf Usmani

ISBN: 81-7231-535-X

Reprint Edition- 2004

Published by *Abdul Naeem* for
Islamic Book Service
2241, Kucha Chelan, Darya Ganj, New Delhi-110 002
Ph.: 23253514, 23265380, 23286551, Fax: 23277913
E-mail: ibsdelhi@del2.vsnl.net.in
        islamic@eth.net
Website: www.islamic-india.com

Printed at: *Noida Printing Press,* C-31, Sector-7, Noida U.P.

CONTENTS

1.	Foreword	9
2.	Introduction	13
3.	After the birth of child.	13
4.	Prayers of this blessed occasion	14
5.	*Tahneek.*	15
6.	Hair cutting; Aqeeqah and naming the child.	15
7.	Khatnah or circumcision	16
8.	Breast feeding	16
9.	The child's clothing.	17
10.	Precaution against misfortun	17
11.	Naming the child	18
12	Some *Ahadith* (Sayings) about naming the child	18
13.	Naming after the name of the Holy Prophet ﴾ﷺ﴿	19
14.	Keeping good names	19
15.	How to find a name	21
16.	Frequent Terms	22
17.	Bibliography:	23

A

18.	Male Names	25
19.	Female Names	39

B

20.	Male Names	45
21.	Female Names	49

D

22. Male Names 51
23. Female Names 54

E

24. Male Names 56

F

25. Male Names 56
26. Female Names 59

G

27. Male Names 63
28. Female Names 65

H

29. Male Names 66
30. Female Names 74

I

31. Male Names 78
32. Female Names 82

J

33. Male Names 83
34. Female Names 86

K

35. Male Names 88
36. Female Names 93

L

37. Male Names _____ 96
38. Female Names _____ 97

M

39. Male Names _____ 98
40. Female Names _____ 114

N

41. Male Names _____ 119
42. Female Names _____ 123

P

43. Female Names _____ 130

Q

44. Male Names _____ 128
45. Female Names _____ 130

R

46. Male Names _____ 131
47. Female Names _____ 135

S

48. Male Names _____ 139
49. Female Names _____ 152

T

50. Male Names _____ 162
51. Female Names _____ 167

Islamic Names

U

52. Male Names_____ 171
53. Female Names_____ 172

W

54. Male Names_____ 175
55. Female Names_____ 178

Y

56. Male Names_____ 180
57. Female Names_____ 182

Z

58. Male Names_____ 183
59. Female Names_____ 187
60. Some famous names of the Messenger's of Allah___ 190
61. The names of Al-Ashrah Mubshsharah_____ 190
62. The names of the wives of the Holy
Prophet _____ 191
63. Names of the children of the Holy Prophet __ 191
64. Daughters._____ 192
65. The names of the scribes of the *Wahi*,
The divine revelation_____ 192

❋ ❋ ❋

FOREWORD

by
Justice Maulana Muhammad Taqi usmani

بسم الله الرحمن الرحيم

الحمدلله وكفى وسلام على عباده الذين اصطفى

To choose a suitable name for a child has always been a matter of interest for a Muslim family. Whenever a child is born, his parents search for a good name for him. Islamic teachings have also encouraged the Muslims to select a meaningful and good name for their children. The Holy Prophet ﷺ has changed the names of several persons, because they carried bad sense.

It is reported by 'Abdullah ibn 'Umar رضى الله عنه , the well-known sahabi, that one of his sisters was named عَاصِيه ('aṣiyah) which means 'disobedient'. The Holy Prophet ﷺ changed her name to 'Jamilah' (beautiful).

Many scientists today have admitted that the name of a person may influence his life, but the Holy Prophet ﷺ has revealed this fact to his followers 1400 years ago when he advised the Muslims to select good names for their children.

The names are also a source of identity of one s religion. Therefore, the Muslims have been naming their children after the prophets, the *Sahabah* (Companions of the Holy Prophet ﷺ) and the pious persons of the Islamic history. Their names have thus been reflecting their Islamic identity.

Unfortunately, this aspect of our lives is being neglected by many Muslims who do not bother to pay any attention to the meaning or any other association attached to their names. In their eagerness to follow the modern trends, they sometimes select a name for their children which is totally meaningless or carrries a bad meaning or has an un-Islamic background.

For example, the female names like 'Tahmina', 'Rubina', 'Nazli' have no meaning at all. The word 'Naaheed' means a woman whose breasts are fully developed, and it is a shame to call a woman with this name. Similarly, some Muslim girls are named as 'Naazilah' which means 'calamity'. Many boys are named as 'parvaiz' while 'Parvaiz' was the name of a King of Persia who had torn the letter of the Holy Prophet ﷺ into pieces. It is shameful for a Muslim to name his child after such an enemy of Islam. It is also seen in some Arab countries that a person is named ' 'Fir'aun' which is the Arabic title of Pharaoh, the tyrant of Egypt who persecuted the followers of Sayyidna Moosa (Moses) عليه السلام

, and was drowned in the sea as a divine punishment.

Some names found in our community are not correct, because they are based on superstitions or on a false belief. The names like 'Ghaws Bakhsh' or 'Rasool Bakhsh' are sometimes adopted to indicate that this child is a gift given by a prophet or a sufi. This belief may be tentamount to *Shirk,* because it is only Allah Almighty who can give a child. Nobody else has any such power.

Sometimes the names are abbreviated in a manner that their accurate sense is totally changed and they fall in the ambit of *Shirk.* For example, the compound names like 'Abdurrahman', 'Abdurrazzaq', 'Abdurrabb', are often abbreviated as 'Rahman', Razzaq' and 'Rabb' while 'Rahman', 'Razzaq' and 'Rabb' are the holy names of Allah which are exclusive for Him alone and cannot be used for any other person. It is not permissible to call a human being with these names without a prefix of 'Abd' etc. But few people attend to this prohibition.

In short, the selection of names for the children should not be taken lightly. It may bring serious results both in this world and in the Hereafter.

However, the Muslims who are consious of this fact need a guide-book which can help them in selecting a suitable name for their children. Some brief booklets are found to serve this purpose, but a more comprehensive book was still needed, specially for the Muslims living in .the Western countries.

On my request, my son Mr. Muhammad Imran Ashraf Usmani who is a graduate of Darul-Uloom Karachi undertook this task and compiled the present guide-book to fulfill this need. He has collected the suitable names for the Muslim boys and girls from the original Arabic resources, and has explained their meanings and their associations. All the names are arranged in an alphabetical order and if some names are non-Arabic, their origin has been indicated before each. Where no such indication is found, it means that they are of Arabic origin.

This is a good collection of the suitable names which is easy to consult. It is hoped that it will assist the English knowing Muslims in acquainting themselves with good Muslim names and their meanings. May Allah bless this effort with His approval and may make it useful for the Muslims and a source of His pleasure in the Hereafter.

This is also the first book of my son Mr. Muhammad Imran Ashraf Usmani which reflects his literary interest. May Allah grant him a long peaceful life and make this book his first step towards a brilliant academic future and a prologue to numerous greater services to Islam and Muslims.

Muhammad Taqi Usmani
Karachi, 27 Muharram 1416 A.H.

INTRODUCTION

الْحَمْدُ لله وَ كَفَىٰ و سَلامٌ على عِبَادِه الّذِين اصْطَفَىٰ،
اللّهُمَّ صَلِّ على سَيِّدنا و مَوْلانا مُحَمَّد و بارِك وسلِّم.

It is indeed a happy occasion and pleasant moment
when parents are blessed with a child. However the real
pleasure can be achieved and enhanced even more if the
rules of Shari'ah are adhered to and all meaningless traditions, rituals and customs are abondoned, which have not
been approved by the Shariah; Almighty Allah has com-
manded us to act upon all the rules which have been mentioned in the Holy Qur'an or laid down by the Holy
prophet ﷺ or practiced by the blessed companions of
the Holy prophet ﷺ.

Therefore, before embarking upon the main subject
of this guide-book, I would like to give a brief account of
some important rules of Sari'ah in this respect. may Almighty Allah give us all the *Tawfeeq* to act upon all the
rules of Sharia'h..

AFTER THE BIRTH OF CHILD:

The first thing that parents should do is to give the
child a Ghusl (Islamic Bath).

Then, the parents should request an Aalim or a pious

person to give Azaan in the right ear and Iqamat in the child's left-ear . It is better that this noble worship (*'Ibaadat*) is undertaken by an Aalim or a pious person so that the Barakat (Blessing of Allah) can be conveyed to the infant , and in the absence of such people, this *'Ibadat* may be performed by any other Muslim.

The benefit of giving Azaan and Iqaamat is that the voice of Islaam, the Greatness of Allah, the Oneness of Allah, and the message of the Holy prophet ﴿ﷺ﴾ will reach to the depth of his heart and he is likely to grow up as a practicing,, obeying Muslim.(انشا ءالله تعالى)

PRAYERS OF THIS BLESSED OCCASION:

It is *mustahab* (better) to recite the following du'aa after the azaan and *iqaamat*:

اللهم إنّي أعيذُها بكَ وَ ذُرِّيَّتَها منَ الشّيطان الرّجيم

O Allah, I seek your protection for ger and ger descendants from the cursed Satan.

Note: For boys read: أعيذهُ and وذُرِّيَّتَهُ

بسم الله الرّحمـن الرّحيم ، قُلْ هُوَ الله أحدٌ ، اللهُ الصَّمَدُ ، لَمْ يَلدْ وَ لَمْ يُولَدْ وَ لمْ يَكُنْ لهُ كُفُواً أحَد

In the name of Allah , the most Beneficient, the most merciful. Say! He is Allah, the One, Allah is one on whom depends the entire creation and He depends on no one. He begetteth not, nor is He begotten. And there is none akin to Him.

اللهُمَّ اجعلهُ برّاً تَقيّاً وَ أنبِتْهُ في الإسلام نَباتاً حَسنًا

O Allah, make him pious and God-fearing and make him grow up in Islaam with an excellent growth.

For girls read:

اللَّهُمَّ اجْعلهَا بَرَّا تقيَّةً وَ أنبِتها في الإسْلام نَبَاتاً حَسَنًا

O Allah, make her pious and God-fearing and
make her grow with an excellent growth.

اللَّهُمَ علِّمهُ الكتَابَ وَ الحكمةَ وَ فقِّههُ في الدِّين.

O Allah, teach him the Qur'an and wisdom
and give him the understanding in Deen.

for girls read:

اللهم علِّمهَا الكتَابَ وَ الحكمةَ وَ فقِّههَا في الدِّين.

O Allah, teach her the Qur'an and wisdom
and give her the understanding in Deen.

TAHNEEK:

Tahneek means: Placing a chewed piece of morsel in
the mouth of an infant, preferably dates. Honey may be
an ideal substitute for it.

Since the Holy prophet ﷺ made the Tahneek of
two companions namely Abdullah Ibne Zubair and Abdullah Ibne Talha (رضي الله تعالى عنهما); this practice of Tahneek has become *Masnoon* (the practice of the Holy
prophet ﷺ) and like Azan this *'Ibadah* should be performed by a learned Aalim or a pious elder of the family;
and in the absence of these people any male Muslim may
do it.

HAIR CUTTING; AQEEQAH AND NAMING THE CHILD:

It is *masnoon* (preferable) to have the baby's head-
shaved, which is termede in Shari'ah as *'Aqeeqah* (First
shaving the head) and to sacrifice an animal and to name
the child on the seventh day after his birth.

After cutting the hair of the child , his removed hair should be weighed and some money equivalent to the weight of the child's hair should be given in charity (as Sadaqah) to the needy people in or out of the family; then the hair should be buried .

For the purpose of *'Aqeeqah* on this occasion two sheep or two goats for a boy and one sheep or one goat for a girl should be sacrificed; and its meat can be eaten by the parents and the family or can be distributed to the poor and needy people.

It should be kept in mind that it is not mandatory to sacrifice two goats or sheep; if the parents cannot afford they can sacrifice one goat or one sheep or they can co-tribute 1/7th of a cow for a girl or 2/7th for a boy, if other partners ar available either performing *Aqeeqah* of their own chidren or performing annual sacrifiece in *Zul-hijjah*.

It is better to recite this *dua'* (prayer) on the occasion of sacrifice :

اللهم هَذا عَقيقَةُ فُلانٍ دَمُها بدمه وَ لَحمُهَا بلحمه و عَظمُهَا بعَظمه وَ جلدَهَا بجلده و شَعرُها بشَعره ، اللهم أجعلهَا فداء إبْني منَ النَّارِ بسم اللهِ، اللهَ أكبر.

KHATNAH OR CIRCUMCISION:

Khatnah (Circumcision) before the age of seven is also a *Sunnah* (preferable practice) in Islam. The child's health must be taken into consideration before deciding to do Khatnah.

BREAST FEEDING:

Since the infant is an offspring of the mother, it is

her moral duty to feed the child. The mother's milk is the most nutritious food for the child. The mother's milk nourishes the child physically and psychologically; it influences his character, habits and senses; it strengthens the bonds of love, affection and intimacy between mother and child; It has other countless benefits also, therefore all other artificial methods should be given up unless mother's health or other circumstances do not allow her to breast feed. However she should always make sure that no *Haram food* (prohibited in Islam) is consumed by the child.

The *Dhikr* and *Bismillah* should always be recited before the feeding.

The maximum period of breast-feeding is two years. Islam does not allow to exceed this period.

THE CHILD'S CLOTHING:

Muslim males are restricted from dressing themselves like women, this is why their male children should not be dressed with silk,or deep red colored clothes and they should not wear gold.

Parents should ensure that the children's dress is in an honorable and modest manner, never imitating the styles of disbelievers.

PRECAUTION AGAINST MISFORTUNE:

In order to Protect the chileren from physical and spiritual ills and to make them immune from Satanic influence,the following *dua* should be recited as often as possible and be blown on the child:

أعوذُ بكلماتِ اللهِ التَّامّاتِ مِن شرِّ كلِّ شيطانٍ و هامَّة

و مِن شَرِّ كل عينٍ لامّة.

> I seek protection by the perfect words of Al-
> lah from the evil of every devil and reptile,
> and from the evil of every revengeful eye.

Aayatul Kursi and the four Quls may also be recited and blown on the child.

NAMING THE CHILD:

It is the infant's vested right to be honored with a good name.While choosing a name for the child, it should be remembered that names may influence the lives of a child . Here are some sayings (*Ahadeeth*) of the Holy prophet ﴾ﷺ﴿ to show the importance of selecting a good and correct name:

SOME AHADITH (SAYINGS) ABOUT NAMING THE CHILD:

عن ابن عمر رضي الله عنه قال قال رسول الله ﴾ﷺ﴿
أحب الأسماء ، إلى الله تعالى عبدالله و عبدالرحمان
(أخرجه مسلم و الترمذي و أبو داؤد).

> Ibn Umar (RA) narrates that the Holy proph-
> et ﴾ﷺ﴿ said: " Truly, the most loved of your
> names by Allah are Abdullah and Abdur-
> Rahmaan."

عن وهب الجشمي قال قال رسو الله ﴾ﷺ﴿: تسموا
بأسماء الأنبياء، و أحب الأسماء إلى الله تعالى: عبدالله
و عبدالرحمن، و أصدقها حارث و همام ، و أقبحها حَرْب و
مُرّه (أخرجه أبوداؤد و النسائي).

> It is also reported that the Holy Prophet

◆ ﷺ ◆ said: Keep the names after the prophets. And the most desirable names by Allah
Almighty are Abdullah and Abdur-Rahmaan,
the most tuthful names are Haarith (planter)
and Hammmaam (thoughtful) And the most
disliked ones are Harb (battle) and Murrah
(bitter).

NAMING AFTER THE NAME OF THE HOLY PROPHET ◆ ﷺ ◆ :

عن ابن جشيب عن أبيه قال قال رسول الله ﴿ ﷺ ﴾ : من
تسمى باسمي يرجو بركتي غدت عليه البركة و راحت إلى
يوم القيامة (كنز العمال برواية أبي نعيم).

The Holy Prophet ◆ ﷺ ◆ said:" whoever is
named after me with the hope of being
blessed, he will be blessed every morning and
evening till the Day of qiyaaamah (Dooms
day)."

عن أبى أمامة قال قال رسول الله ﴿ ﷺ ﴾: مَن وُلِدَ لـه
مولودٌ ذكرُ فسمّاه محمداً حبّاً لي و تبركاً باسمي كا · هو و
مولوده في الجنة. (كنز العمال برواية الرافعي).

He ◆ ﷺ ◆ also said: " To whomever is born a
boy and he names him Muhammad only out
of love for me and for the blessings of my
name , then both he (the father) and his son
will be in Jannah(Paradise)."

KEEPING GOOD NAMES:

عن أبي الدرداء قال قال رسول الله ﴿ ﷺ ﴾: إنكم تدعـون يوم القيامة
بأسمائكم و أسماء آبائكم ، فأحسنوا أسمائكم . (أخرجه أبو داؤد)

The Holy prophet ◆ ﷺ ◆ said: On the Day of

Qiyamah you will be called by your (own) names and the names of your fathers. Therefore keep good names." (Aboo Dawood)

عن أبي هريرة قال قال رسول الله ﴿ ﷺ ﴾: حق الولد على
والده أن يحسن إسمه و يزوجه إذا أدرك ، و يعلمه الكتاب
(ذكره ابو نعيم في حلية الأولياء و الديلمي في مسند
الفردوس ، كنز العمال) .

The Holy prophet ﴿ ﷺ ﴾ said: It is the right of a child that his father should give him a good name; and when he becomes of age should get him married; and he should give him the education of Quraan."

It was the practice of the Holy prophet ﴿ ﷺ ﴾ to inquire the names of persons and villages. If they were pleasant, it became apparent on his face. If not, his displeasure could be seen.

عن أبي سعيد القطان أن رسول الله ﴿ ﷺ ﴾ قال للقحة
تحلب : من يحلب هذه؟ فـقـام رجل، فـقـال له رسـول الله
﴿ ﷺ ﴾: مـا إسمك ؟ فـقـال له الرجل : حرب، فـقـال له
رسـول الله ﴿ ﷺ ﴾: إجلس، ثم قال: من يحلب هذه؟ فقام
رجل، فـقـال له رسـول الله ﴿ ﷺ ﴾: مـا اسمك ؟ فـقـال:
يعـيش، فـقـال له رسـول الله ﴿ ﷺ ﴾: أحلب . (أخـرجـه
الموطا)

Once the Holy prophet ﴿ ﷺ ﴾ called for a person to milk a camel. One person volunteered; the Holy Prophet ﴿ ﷺ ﴾ said to him: What is your name? he said: Harb, the Holy Prophet ﴿ ﷺ ﴾ said: Sit down and refused to accept his service because his name was Harb(meaning: War) which did not imply pleasantness. Then the second person stood up to milk, the Holy Prophet ﴾ﷺ﴿ asked him his name; he said: Ya'eesh(يعيش long live). The Holy Prophet ﴾ﷺ﴿ said to him: "Milk her".

The Holy Prophet ﴾ﷺ﴿ used to change bad names as the following *Hadith* tells us:

عن عائشة رضي الله عنها قالت : أن رسول الله ﴾ﷺ﴿ كان يغير الإسم القبيح . (أخرجه الترمذي رقم: ٢٨٣١)

A'aisha (رضي الله عنها) narrates that the Holy Prophet ﴾ﷺ﴿ used to change bad names.

HOW TO FIND A NAME:

The names in this book have been collected from the original Arabic resources, and have been explained with regard to their meanings and their associations. All the names are arranged in an alphabetical order and if some names are non-Arabic, their origin has been indicated before each. Where no such indication is found, it means that they are of Arabic origin.

According to the rules of transliteration, the Arabic Alphabets will be found as under:

ت under the chapter of T

ث ---------------------- TH

ح ---------------------- Ḥ

خ ---------------------- KH

ذ ---------------------- DH

ز ---------------------- Z

س	S
ش	SH
ص	S
ض	D
ط	T
ظ	ZH
ع	'A
ع	'I
ع	'U
غ	GH
ق	Q
ك	K
و	W
ة	H
ي	Y

However, for the convenience of a common reader not acquainted with this transliteration scheme, the names are arranged according to their pronunciation also. For example, the name ثابت can be found in the chapter of **T** (as 'Thaabit') and also in the chapter of **S** (as Saabit) the name ذاكر can he found in the chapter of **D** (as Dhaakir) as well as in t he chapter of **Z** (as Zaakir) and so on. That is why some names may be found in more than one place.

Frequent Terms:

There are some terms frequently used in the book. Here is their brief explanation:

Sahabi: A male companion of the Holy Prophet 🕌 who

has the honour of seeing him in the state of Islam. Pl.
Ṣahabah.

Ṣahaabiyyah: A female companion of the Holy Prophet
ﷺ.

Taabi'i : A pupil of a Ṣahabi.

Taabi'iyyah : A female pupil of a Ṣahabi.

Raawi: A person who has reported some traditions of the
Holy Prophet ﷺ.

Raawiyah: A female reporter of the traditions.

Hadith: A saying or a tradition of the Holy Prophet ﷺ
Pl. Aḥadith.

Muḥaddith: A person qualified in the science of hadith.

Mujaahid: A one who fights for an Islamic cause.

Quari: A scholar of the science of recitation of the Holy
Qur'an.

BIBLIOGRAPHY:

The names in this book are taken from the Arabic,
Persian, English and Urdu authentic books; the names of
the books are listed below:

(١):تقريب التهذيب للحافظ ابن حجر العسقلاني(رحمه الله) .

(٢): الإصابه في معرفة الصحابه للحافظ ابن حجر العسقلاني(رحمه الله)

(٣):الإستيعاب في معرفة الأصحاب لإبن عبد البر القرطبي .

(٤):أعلام النسآء لكحاله عمر رضا.

(٥):إسلامي نام (اردو، مولف: محمد مختار).

(٦):الأعلام للزّركلي .

(٧):المغني للعلامة الهندي.

(٨):الأسماء الحسنى لمحمد إسماعيل زكريا.

(٩)أسماء البدريين للمفتي محمد شفيع (رحمه الله).

(١٠):الأنساب للسمعاني .

(١١):سير اعلام النبلاء للذهبي.

(١٢):أسماء الخلفاء والولاة لابن حزم.

(١٣):جامع الأصول لابن أثير.

(١٤):كنز العمال لعلاءالدين علي المتقي الهندي.

(١٥): جوامع السيرة لابن حزم.

(15): Names for Muslim children (English)compiled by Qari Muhammad Rafiq.

In the last, I request all the readers of this book to remember me and my parents in their *duaas*. May Allah grant His approval to my this little effort and bless me with the guidance to render more and greater services to Islam and Muslims.

وما توفيقي إلا بالله، عليه توكلت و إليه أنيب.

Muhammad Imran Ashraf Usmani

14 Safar 1416 A.H.

> Note: When a child is given a name where one of the attributes of Allah is desired to be used it is necessary that the word Abd meaning servant or slave be used as a prefix; as Abdullah, AbdulBaari, meaning the servant of Allah or the Creator Deity.

'Aabid: عابد

Worshipper; Suitable combination: Muhammad 'Aabid, 'Aabidurrahmaan.

'Aadil: عادل

Just; upright; sincere; attribute of the Holy prophet ﴾ﷺ﴿.

'Aalam: عالم

World suitble combination: Muhammad Aalam, Fakhr 'Alam.

'Aali: عالی

Sublime , high.

'Aalim : عالم

Scholar , knowing,

'Aamil: عامل

Doer , work man.

'Aamir: عامر

Inhabited; populous; full;filled up; cultivated (of

land); civilized; flourishing; prosperous.

'Aaqib: عاقب
Suckered, follower.

'Aaqil: عاقل
Intelligent.

'Aarif: عارف
Knowing, skilled, recognizing Allah .

'Aashir: عاشر
living; spending a life.

'Aashiq: عاشق
Lover.

'Aasif: آصف
It was the name of the minister of Hazrat Sulaimaan, the prophet of Allah .

'Aasim: عاصم
Keeper, guardian, protector; name of a famous
Quari.

'Aatif: عاطف
Kind, affectionate; compassionate.

'Aatiq: عاتق
Free; liberated; independent; Name: Aatiq Ali;
Muhammad Aatiq.

'Azeem : عظيم
('Aazheem)Great.

A'zham : اعظم
(Aazam) Greatest.

'Aazim: عازم
intending; determining; resolved on; applying the mind to an undertaking.

Abaan: ابان
Name of a great Muahaddith ,scholar of Hadith.

'Abbaad: عبّاد
Great worshipper.

'Abbaas: عباس
The uncle of the Holy prophet and well-known Sahabi.

'Abdul-Ahad: عبدالأحد
Slave of the One; unique; without prtner; *Al Ahad* is one of the attributes of Almighty Allah.

'Abdul-Khaaliq: عبدالخالق
Slave of the Creator; one who creates things from non - existence.

'Abdullah: عبدالله
slave of Allah; favorite name of the Holy prophet ﴾ﷺ﴿.

'Abdul-Qayyoom: عبدالقيوم
Slave of the Everlasting; *Al Qayyom* is an attribute excessively applied to Allah Almighty.

'Abdul-Quahhaar: عبدالقهّار

Slave of the The Subduing; He who is victorious and dominant in a way that He can do anything He wills.

'Abdul-Qadeer: عبدالقدير

Slave of the Powerful; mighty.

'Abdul-Quddoos: عبدالقدوس

Slave of the One who is free from any physical and moral defects; blessed; pious; and celestial person; Quddoos is an attribute applied to Allah.

'Abdur-Rabb: عبدالرب

Slave of the the Sustainer; master.

'Abdus-Samad: عبدالصمد

Slave of the Eternal; Slave of the One who is need-free and the only being to apply to if one has any need to be completed or any troubles to be eliminated.

'Abdus-Sattaar: عبدالستار

Slave of the One who conceals faults by the veil of His Mercy.

'Abdul-Wahhab: عبدالوهاب

Slave of the One who gives charity etc. abundantly.

'Abdur Rahmaan: عبدالرحمان

Slave of Rahmaan, the Most beneficent; the Holy prophet(peace be upon him) liked this name for a Muslim child.

Aboo Mahdhoorah: ابو محذوره

> (Abu mahzoorah) Name of one companion of the prophet of Allah.

Abraar: ابرار

> Pl. of birr: virture, piety.

Abtahi: ابطحى

> One who lives in Abtah, a place near Makkah.

Abu Ayyoub: ابو ايوب

> Popular Sahabi of the prophet of Allah; when the Holy prophet, peace be upon him, migrated to Madinah, He hosted him in his home for some days.

Abu Darda': ابو درداء:

> Famous Sahabi of Rasoolullah, peace be upon him.

Abudhar: ابوذر

> (Abu zarr) A great Sahabi of the prophet of Allah.

Abu taalib: ابو طالب

> The uncle of the Holy prophet peace be upon him; and the father of Hazrat Ali (R.H).

Abubakr: ابو بكر

> Famous Sahabi; First Caliph of the Prophet ﷺ

Abuhanifa: ابو حنيفه

> A great scholar and jurist of Islamic law.

Abuhudhaifah: ابو حذيفه

(Abu huzaifah) A faomous Sahabi of Rasoolullah,peace be upon him.

Abuhurairah: ابو هريره

A greaat Sahabi who is the narrator of many
Ahadith (traditions).

Abujuhafah: ابوجحيفه

A Sahabi of the Holy prophet peac be upon him.

Abul haitham: ابوالهيثم

(Abul haitham) A Sahabi; also a great scholar of
history.

Abulkalaam: ابوالكلام

A great scholar, wellknown politician .

Abulyusr: ابو اليُسر

A great Sahabi who particepated in the battle of
Badr.

Abu Mas'ood: ابو مسعود

A great Sahabi who particepated in the battle of
Badr.

Abu Moosa: ابو موسى

A well-knowh Sahabi; his full name was Abu
Moosa Al Ash'ari.

Abu Saeed: ابو سعيد

A well-known Sahabi; his full name was Abu
sa'eed Khudri.

AbuTalḥa: ابو طلحه

A great Sahabi who particepated in the battle of
Badr.

AbuTuraab: ابو تراب

One of the names of Hazrat 'Ali.

Abu 'Ubaidah: ابو عبيده

A great Sahabi of the prophet peace be upon him; One of the ten companions whom the Holy Prophet (Peace be upon him) has declared as the people of Jannah.

Abu Yousuf: ابو يوسف

Name of a great jurist and pupil of Imaam Abu Hanifah (RA).

Aadam: آدم

The first prophet of Allah; and first human being sent to the earth.

Adeeb: اديب

Literary person.

'Adeel: عديل

Equal; Like.

'Adi: عدى

A Sahabi of the prophet of Allah; and son of Haatim Taai,a Person famous for his in generosity ; full name was 'Adiyy ibn Haatim.

'Adl: عدل

Justice.

'Adnaan: عدنان

Name of a leader of the tribe of Quraish. The Holy prophet ﴾ﷺ﴿ was from this tribe.

Afdaal: افضال

(Afzaal)Plu, of Fazl, superiority.

Afdal: افضل

(Afzal) Superior and excellent.

'Afeef: عفيف

Pure; chaste; virtuous; modest; holy in life; of spotless character.

Aflah: افلح

Having much prosperity and success in the world and hearafter.

'Afuww: عفوّ

The Pardoner; He who pardons all who repent sincerely as if they had no previous sin. It is an attribute of Allah; therefore the best combination is AbdulAffuww.

Afzaal: افضال

(Afdaal) Plu, of Fazl, superiority.

Afzal: افضل

(Afdal) Superior and excellent.

Ahad: احد

The One; the best name is AbdulAhad.

Ahmar: احمر

Red coloured.

Ahmad: احمد

Name of the last prophet of Allah (ﷺ).

Ajmal: اجمل

The most beautiful ; pretty.

Ajwad: اجود

More generous; bountifull; magnificent; gracious.

Akbar: اكبر

Bigger.

Akhlaaq: اخلاق

Plu. of Khuluq, Behavior; comportment; conduct; deportmement.

Akhtar: اختر

(Persian) A star; a constellation; good omen; good luck; good fortune.

Akmal: اكمل

More complete; more perfect; integral.

Akram: اكرم

Nobler; more distinguished; more precious; most honorable; most generous.

'Alaa: علاء

Hieght; elevation; high rank; nobility; loftiness; sublimity.

'Aleem: عليم

The All knowing, He who has all knowledge. Name: AbduAleem.

'Ali: علي

The Most High, He who is the highest ; an attribute applied to Allah; Name of famous copanion of the prophet, peace be upon him, Suitable combination: Abaul Ali; Muhammad Ali.

Amaan: امان

Safety; security; immunity; quarter; grace; mercy; protection.

Ameen: امين

Safe; secure; reliable; honest; trustworthy; faithful; loyal ; (authorized) reprsentative or agent; trustee; superintendent; keeper; custodian; head-chief; chamberlain.

Ameer: امير

Cmmander; emir; prince; commander of the Faithfull; caliph.

'Ammaar: عمّار

One who inhabits a place having long life; A famous Sahabi known as Ammaar ibn Yaasir.

'Amr: عَمر

Life (of a person; used in oaths only); A famous Sahabi known as Amr ibn Al Aas.

Anas: انس

A great Sahabi of the Holy prophet (peace be upon him) many traditions are narratted by him.

Anees: انيس

Intimate; friendly; sociable; civil; polite; close; intimate friend.

Anwaar: انوار

(Plu of Noor) Lights; brightnesses; glow;gleams.

Anwar: انور

Brighter; Luminous; radiant; shininig; enlighten-
ing.

'Aqeel: عقيل

A wise and intelligent man; a sensible man.

Areeb: اريب

Skillful; adroit.

Arqam: ارقم

Pen; speckled snack; and name of a Sahabi
known as Arquam ibn abi Arquam.

Arsalaan: ارسلان

(Turkish) Lion.

Arshad: ارشد

Rightly guided; having the true faith; soberer;
grave; most conscious; most sensible; intelligent;
of full legal age.

Arshaq: ارشق

Handsome; one with a befitting height and a
well-proportioned body.

As'ad: اسعد

Happier; more lucky; gladder; felicitous; fortunate.

Asad: اسد
>   Lion.

Asbagh: اصبغ
>   Colored animal; a huge flood; dyer.

Asghar : اصغر
>   Shorter; smaller; tiniest;more diminutive.

Ash'ab: اشعب
>   Lion; difficult; strict.

Asha'ath: اشعث
>   (Asha'as) Scattered;spread about irregularly, humble.

Ashfaaq: اشفاق
>   (Pl. of Shafaq) Evenining twiilght.

Ashraf: اشرف
>   Nobler; more eminent; more honorable; a great scholar named Ashraf Ali Thaanvi.

'Askar: عسكر
>   Troop.

Aslam: اسلم
>   Safer; more free; sounder; healthier.

'Ata': عطاء
>   Grant; Donation.

'Ateeq: عتيق
>   Old; antique; aged; free, emancipated.

Athar: اطهر

Cleaner/ Cleanest; pure; spotless.

Atyab: اطيب

Great; fine; nice; noble; better/ best.

'Aauf: عوف

Name of A Sahabi.

Aaus: أوس

Name of a number of Sahabah, e.g. Aus ibn Thabit; Aus ibn Saamit Aus ibn kholy.

'Aun : عون

Helping..

Awwal: أول

(Al Awwal): the First; Name: AbdulAwwal.

Ayman: ايمن

Right; right hand; on the right; lucky.

Ayyoob: ايوب

(Ayyub)A famous prophet of Allah; Ayyoob's equivalent in English is 'Job'.

'Azeem: عظيم

(Adheem): Great; big, large.

Azhar: أزهر

White; glittering; blooming; a face full of light.

Azh'har: اظهر

More visible; distinct; obvious; clear; evident.

'Aziz: عزيز

> Dear; beloved; respected; esteemed; precious; powerful; rare; an attribute of Allah Almighty Name: AbdulAzeez.

'Azhmat: عظمت

> Greatness; Largeness; bigness; magnitude; amplitude.

Female Names

'Aabidah: عابده

Worshipper.

'Aabirah: عابره

Passer by ; fragrant.

Aafrin: آفرین

(Persian): Appreciation.

'Aaisha: عائشه

Beloved wife of the prophet of Allah. Meaning : Well living woman .

'Aakifah: عاكفه

A lady who worships Allah in solitude.

'Aaliah : عاليه

Sublime , high woman.

'Aalimah: عالمه

Woman scholar

'Aamilah: عامله

A woman; doing good deeds.

Aamina: آمنه

Secured ,safe woman: the mother of the Holy Prophet (Peace be upon him)

'Aamirah: عامره

A woman inhabitig in a place.

Aanisah: آنسه

> Young lady; virgin; unmarried or chaste woman; intact; maiden; friendly.

'Aaqilah: عاقله

> Intelligent woman.

'Aarifah: عارفه

> Knowing, skilled, recognizing Allah .

Aarzoo: آرزو

> (Urdu word) desire, wish.

'Aasimah: عاصمه

> A woman who saves others .

Aasiyah: آسیه

> Pharaoh's wife who embraced Islam .

'Aatikah: عاتکه

> Name of one of the companions of the Holy-prophet of Allah(Peace be upon him).

'Aatiqah: عاتقه

> Emancipated; a beautiful lady; of honourable family back ground.

'Aatirah: عاطره

> Of good fragrance; a connoisseur of fragrance.

'Abqurah: عبقره

> Name of a Sahabiyah.

Ada: ادا

> (Urdu word) To perform; grace;elegance;

charm.

'Adhraa': عذرآء

(Azraa') Young lady; virgin; unmarried or chaste woman; intact; maiden.

'Afeefah: عفيفه

Pure; chaste; virtuous; modest; holy in life; of spotless character.

'Afeerah: عفيره

Covered with dust of a dusty colour name of A Sahabiyah who participated in the war of Yarmook .

'Afraa': عفرآء

Name of a Sahabiyyah.

Afroze: افروز

(Persian)) Brightening.

Afshan: افشان

(Persian) : Small golden particles used by women to adorne their face and hair.

'Aleemah: عليمه

knowing, scholar, very learned woman.

Almaas: الماس

A diamond.

'Ammaarah: عمّاره

Name of a Sahaabi.

Amah: امة

> A female servant; a female slave; a handmaid; a maid servant.

Amatullah: امة الله

> Maid servant of Allah.

'Amber: عنبر

> Ambergris.

Ameenah: أمينه

> Trust worthy; faithful; honest.

Amirah: اميره

> Princess.

'Amrah: عمره

> Head gear; turban; (Egypt.) repair work; name of a Sahabiyah.

Aneesah: انيسه

> Compapnion; an affectionate friend; name of a Sahaabi.

Angbin: انگبین

> (Persian word): Honey

'Anizah: عنيزه

> She goat.

Anjum : النجم

> (Persian) Star.

'Aqueelah: عقيله

A wise and intelligent woman; a sensible woman.

Aribah: أريبه

Skillful woman.

Arjumand: ارجمند

(Persian) Honorable; noble; worthy; blessed; possessing dignity; dear.

Arwaa: اروا

The aunt (father's sister) of the Holy prophet peace be upon him.

Asmaa': اسماء

Heights; Name of a Sahabiyyah, the daughter of Hazrat Abu Bakar Siddique; and the mother of Abdullah ibn zubair.

Athilah: اثيله

(Asilah) Strengthened; consolidated.

'Atiquah : عتيقه

(Feminine of Atique) Old; antique; free Old woman; a noble woman; a free woman.

'Atiyyah: عطيه

Grant; Donation; gift.

'Azheemah: عظيمه

(Azeemah): Great; encomassing; dignified.

'Azeezah: عزيزه

Dear; respected; esteemed; precious; rare; powerful.

'Azra': عذراء

('Adhraa') Young lady; virgin; unmarried or chaste woman; intact; maiden.

 ☆ ☆ ☆

ب

Baahir: باهِر
Prevailing.

Baaqi: باقی
The Everlasting; perpetual ; an attribute of Allah
.Name: Abdul-Baaqi.

Baari: باری
Creator, one of the attributes of Almighty Allah.

Baarr: بارّ
Just; pious.

Baasim: باسِم
Smiling; happy.

Baasit: باسط
Conferrer of prosperity ; one of the attributes of
Allah. Name: Abdul-Baasit.

Baatin: باطن
Inner; hidden; secret; internal.

Baayazeed: بایزید
The name of a king known as Baayazeed Yalda-
rim; also the name of a great sufi.

Baatin: باطن
Inner; hidden; secret; internal.

Badr: بدر
Full moon.

Badee': بديع

(Badi') Novel, Strange, Rare;one of the Attributes of Allah . Name, Abdul-Badee'.

Baha': بهآء.

Beauty; elegance; exellence; it also means in Persian: value; Names: Bahaa'uddeen; Bahaa'ulhaq.

Bahhath: بحاث

Name of a great Sahabi (R.A) who participated in the battle of Badr .

Baleegh: بليغ

Eloquent; learned.

Baleel: بليل

Name of a Sahabi who was present in the battle of Uhud.

Baqir: باقر

Well learned; fierce; lion; a very wealthy man; the title of Imam Aboo Ja'far.

Baraa': براء

Name of a Sahabi(R.A).

Baree': برى

Free; Free from the Hell.

Barakat: بركت

Blessing.

Barr: بَرّ

Just; pious. Name of Sahabi who was present in the battle of Badr and Name of a Raaviyah.

Baseer: بصير

Wise; sagacious; Allah's attribute; Name: Abdul-Baseer; Baseer Ahmed.

Bashaarat: بشارت

Good news; forecast; glad tidings.

Basheer: بشير

Bearer of good news.

Basrah: بصره

Name of a sahabiyyah; dry land.

Bassaam: بسّام

Frequently smiling; Name of a Raavi of Hadith.

Batin: باطن

The Hidden; Allah's attribute.

Bilaal: بلال

Name of a famous Sahabi who recited Azaan in the days of the Holy Prophet peace be upon him .

Bin yamin: بن يامين

Son of Yaqoob (Jacob) عليه السلام; Father of one of the twelve tribes of Bani Israaeel.

Bisher: بشر

Happiness; good news; name of a Sahabi known as Bishr al Hafi.

Bujair: بجير

Name of a Sahabi ; A Sahahbi known as Bujair ibn Bujair was present in the battle of Badr .

Buraid: بريد

Name of a Sahabi and Raavi, who narrates the

sayings of the prophet peace be upon him.

Buraidah: بريده

Name of a Sahabi known as Buraidah ibn Husaib(R.A); Name of a place situated in Saudi Arabia.

Burhaan: برهان

Argument; proof; evidence.

Female Names

Baadiyah: باديه
　　Name of a sahabiyyah.

Bahaa': بهآء
　　Beauty; brilliancy; loveliness.

Bahaar: بهار
　　(Persian word) spring; prime; bloom; beauty;
　　glory; elegance; delight; enjoyment; flourishing
　　state; fine landscape.

Bakht: بخت
　　(Persian word):Luck; good fortune; prosperity;
　　lot; portion.

Bakhtaawar: بختاور
　　(Persian)Fortunate; lucky.

Baqilah: باقله
　　Name of a sahabiyyah.

Bareerah: بريره
　　Virtuous; Name of a famous Sahabiyyah.

Barakat: بركت
　　Blessing.

Barrah: برّة
　　Aunt of the Holy prophet (peace be upon him);
　　name of a Sahabiyyah.

Barsa': برصا

Name of a sahabiyyah.

Basbasah: بسبسه

Name of a Sahabi who was present in the battle of Badr and Name of a female narrator of ahadith.

Basheerah: بشيره

Name of a sahabiyyah.

Baaṭinah: باطنه

Name of a sahabiyyah.

Batool: بتول

A virgin; a pure and chaste woman devoted to God (usually applied to Maryam عليه السلام and to Hazrat Fatimah.

Bilqees: بلقيس

A queen of Saba in the days of Hazrat Sulaimaan (عليه السلام) as mentioned in the Holy Qur'an.

Bismah: بسمه

Smile.

Bina: بينا

(Beena) the Persian word; meaning: A person who can see.

Buhaisah: بُحيثه

Name of a sahabiyyah; Name of a Raviyyah, who narrated Hadith.

Bushra: بشرى

Glad tiding; good news.

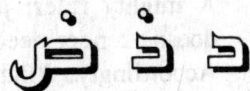

Daamin ضامن
: (Zaamin): One who stands surety for another, one who helps.

Daanish: دانش
: (Persian) Knowledge; science; and learning.

Daanyaal: دانیال
: Name of a prophet of Allah Almighty. Its English equivalent is Daniel.

Dahhaak: ضحاك
: (Zahhaak): Name a of a Sahabi who participated in the battle of Badr.

Dameer: ضمیر
: (Zameer): Heart; conscience.

Damurah: ضمرہ
: (Zamurah) Name of Sahabi who participated in the battle of Badr .

Dawlah: دَولہ
: Riches; happiness; felicity; prosperity; Name: Saifuddawlah.

Dawood: داؤد
: Name of a well-known prophet of Allah Almighty; Its English equivalent is David.

Dayyaan: دیّان

A mighty ruler; judge , protector; one who doesn't render deed worthless but compensates Accordingly, Allah's attribute. Name : Abdud Dayyan.

Deen: دین

Religion.

Dhaakir: ذاکر

(Zaakir) One who constantly praises and remembers Allah Ta'ala..

Dhakaa': ذکاء

(Zakaa) Keen perception; sharpness of mind; deep insight; sagacity. Name: Zakaa' ud-Deen.

Dhakawaan: ذکوان

(Zakawaan) Name of a Sahabi who participated in the battle of Badr.

Dhaki: ذکی

(Zaki) One who has a sharp mind and keen perception; intelligent. Name: Zakiyyud-Deen.

Dheeshaan: ذیشان

(Zeeshaan) Graceful; distinguished, elegant.

Dhulfaqaar: ذوالفقار

(Zulfaqar) Name of a celebrated sword which fell into the hand of Rasoolullah sallallaahu-alayhi- wasallam in the Battle of Badr and which was presented to Ali(RA). Note: It is incorrect to Say Fiqaar (with kasrah).

Dhukaa': ذکاء

The sun ; dawn; morning; suitable combination: Zukaa' uddeen.

Dhulkifl: ذوالكفل
> (Zulkifl) Name of a prophet of Allah.

Dhunnoon: ذوالنون
> (Zunnoon) The title of Hazrat Yoonus (Peace be upon him) meaning The Man of the whale,

Dhushshimalain: ذوالشمالين
> (Zushimalin) Name of a Sahabi (RA).

Dihyah: دحيه
> Name of a Sahabi.

Dilawar: دلاور
> (Persian):Courageous; brave; audacious; bold.

Dildaar: دلدار
> (Persian): Possessing or delighting the heart; charming; beloved; sweetheart.

Diyaa': ضياء
> (Ziyaa) Light; spender; brilliance.

Duhaa: ضحى
> (Zuhaa) Forenoon. Name: Shamsu-Zuhaa.

<hr>

Female Names

Daniyah: دانيه
Dear; close; low; easy; comfortable.

Darakhshaan: درخشان
(Persian): Shining.

Darrah: درّه
Name of a Sahabiyah, daughter of Abu Lahab

Daulah: دَوله
Wealth; government.

Deebaa: ديبا
(Persian): Cloth of silk.

Deenah: دينه
(Arabic): Obedience; nature; habit; Name of a Sahabiyah (RA).

Duba'ah: ضُباعه
(Zuba'ah): Name of a Sahabiyah, Daughter of uncle of the Holy prophet (peace be upon him).

Dhaakirah: ذاكره
One who constantly remembers and glorifies Allah.

Dhakiyah: ذاكيه
A lady with keen perception and a sharp mind; an intelligent lady.

Dhakiyyah: ذكيه

A lady with a sharp mind and keen perception; intelligent.

Dujanah: دجانه

Name of a woman.

Durdaanah : دردانه

A pearl; Name of a woman.

Durrah: درّه

A large or precious pearl; name of a Sahaabi (RA).

E'jaz: اعجاز

To do something which others can not do .

Faaiq: فائق

Superior; excelling; excellent; surpassing.

Faakih: فاكه

Funny; humopous; Name of a Sahabi who took part in the battle of Badr.

Faakhir: فاخِر

Exellent; precious; honourable.

Faaris: فارس

Horseman; rider; knight; cavalier; hero.

Faatih: فاتح

Opener; beginner; conqueror.

Faazil: فاضل

(Faadil): An accomplished person ; a scholar.

Faheem: فهيم

Intelligent; learned; knowing.

Faisal: فيصل

Judge; decided; settled; name of a famous king of Saudi Arabia.

Faiz: فيض
>
> (Faiḍ): Liberality; grace; favour; bounty; abundance.

Faizaan: فيضان
>
> (Faidaan)Beneficence; generosity; abundance; overflow; benefit.

Fakeeh: فكيه
>
> Cheerful; amusing; happy; humourous.

Fakhr: فخر
>
> Glory; pride; a thing to be proud of .

Faoz: فوز
>
> Success; victory; advantage; gain; salvation.

Faqeeh: فقيه
>
> One well versed in religious laws; jurist.

Faraasat: فراست
>
> Perception; discernment; sagacity; understanding; insight.

Faraaz: فراز
>
> (Persian)Ascent; height; elevation. adj. High; aloft; exalted; lofty; exalting; elevating; ascending.

Fareed: فريد
>
> Unique; precious; having no equal; incomparable.

Farhaan: فرحان
>
> Glad; joyful.

Farqad: فرقد
>
> Name of a star; name of a schloar.

Faarooq: فاروق

One who distinguishes between right and wrong; the title of Hazrat Umar, the second Caliph of Islam.

Farrukh: فرخ

Happy; fortunate; auspicious; beautiful.

Faseeh: فصيح

Eloquent.

Fattaah: فتّاح

One who attains victory; an attribute of Allah Almighty . Name: Abdul Fattah.

Fu'aad: فؤاد

The heart.

Fazl: فضل

(Faḍl): Excellence; virtue; superiority; increase; excess; reward; grace; bounty; wisdom.

Fidaa': فداء

Redemption; devoting one's self to save another; ransom; suitable combination for names : Fidaa' ur-Rahmaan; Fida' Muhammad.

Fauzaan: فوزان

Succesful; victorious; advantageous.

Furqaan: فرقان

A criterion (for distinguishing truth from falsehood). Another name for the Qur'aan since it distinguishes truth from falsehood.

Fuzail: فضيل

(Fuḍail): Name of a saint known as Fuzail bin 'Iyaad.

Names of Female

Faadilah: فاضله
(Faazilah): Accomplished; virtuous; accomplished; a female scholar.

Faa'izah: فائزه
Successful; prosperous; victorious.

Faakhirah: فاخره
Elegant; splendid; proud.

Faakihah: فاكهه
Fruits.

Faari'ah: فارعه
Name of a Sahabiyah; Her second name was Furai'ah.

Faarihah: فارهة
A swift she-camel.

Faatihah: فاتحه
Beginning; introduction; preface; opener; conqueror.

Faatimah: فاطمه
The lovely daughter of the Holy Prophet peace be upon him.

Faazilah: فاضله
(Faadilah): Accomplished; virtuous; accomplished; a female scholar.

Fadeelah: فضيله
(Fazeelah): Superiority; attuibute; value.

Faheemah: نهيمه
Intelligent; learned.

Fahmeedah: نهميده
(Persian): Intelligent; wise.

Fakeeaha: نكيهه
Cheerful; amusing; happy; humourous.

Fakhitah: ناخته
A dove; a ringed turtledove; the name of a Sahabiyyah.

Fakhr: نخر
Pride; a thing to be proud of;suitable name: Fakhrun-nisaa'.

Faoz: نوز
Success; victory; advantage; gain; salvation.

Farah: فرح
Joy; gladness; cheerfulness.

Fareedah: نريده
Unique; precious; having no equal; incomparable.

Farhanah: نرحانه
Glad; joyful.

Farhat: نرحت
Delight; pleasure; joy; cheerfulness; amusement; recreation; diversion.

Farihah: فريحه

Happy; pleased.

Farkhandah: فرخنده

(Persian): Happy; fortunate.

Farrukh: فرّخ

Happy; fortunate; auspicious; beautiful.

Farwah: فروه

Fur; Name of a Sahabiyah; and also name of a Sahabi who took part in the battle of Badr.

Faseehah: فصيحه

Eloquent.

Fateenah: فطينه

Intelligent; sagacious.

Fatimah: فاطمه

The lovely daughter of the prophet peace be upon him.

Fauziah: فوزيه

Vitorious; successful; one who has attained salvation.

Fazeelah: فضيله

(Fadeelah): Superiority; attuibute; value.

Feeroozah: فيروزه

A precious stone; Turquoise.

Fiddah: فضّة

(Fizzah); Silver; name of a maid servant of Hazrat Faatimh (RAH).

Firdous: فردوس
>A garden; paradise.

Fizzah: نضّة
>(Fiḍḍah); Silver; name of a maid servant of Hazrat Faatimh (RAH).

Foziah: فوزیه
>(Persian): successful.

Furai'ah: فُریعة
>Name of a Sahabiyah; her second name was Faari'ah.

Fusaila: فُصیلة
>Name of a female narrator of hadith; daughter of Wathilah ibn Asqa', a well known Sahabi.

Ghaalib: غالب
Pre dominant.

Ghazawaan: غزوان
Warrior; name of a sahabi.

Guṭaif: غُطيف
A well of a person; well to do.

Ghailaan: غيلان
Name of a Sahabi and of a scholar of Hadith.

Ghassaan: غسّان
Name of a scholar of Hadith.

Ghaazi: غازى
Warrior.

Ghaffaar: غفار
Allah's attribute meaning: Most Forgiving, Most
Merciful; Name: abdul-Ghaffaar.

Ghaith: غيث
Rain.

Ghani: غنى
(Ghaniyy): The Self sufficient; Name: Abdul
Ghani.

Ghannaam: غنّام
Shepherd; name of a Sahabi who took part in the
battle of Badr.

Ghunaim: غُنيم
Name of a Sahabi.

Ghauth: غوث

(Gaus): Helper or defender.

Ghayyoor: غيور

Self-respecting.

Ghazalaan: غزلان

Spinner.

Ghfoor: غفور

Allah's attribute; meaning: Most Forgiving, Most Merciful. Name: Abdul-Ghafoor.

Ghufraan: غفران

Forgiving; much forgiving (esp. for Allah); to cover; hide.

Ghulaam: غلام

Lad; Slave; servant. Name: Ghulaamullah; Ghulaam Muhammad.

Gohar: گوهر

(Persian)Diamond; precious stone.

Gulaab: گلاب

(Persian): Rose.

Gulfaam: گلفام

(Persian): Red colored; rosy faced.

Gulshan: گلشن

(Persian): A rose or flower garden.

Gul-e-r'anaa: گل رعنا

(Persian): A beautiful flower.

Gulzaar: گلزار

(Persian): A bed of roses; a garden; a well populated town.

Female Names

Ghazalah: غزاله

Female gazelle, doe; (rising) sun; rise of the sun.

Ghareebah: غريبه

Strange; unusual; amazing; rare.

Ghaaziyah:غازيه

Woman warior.

Ghalibah:غالبه

Pre dominant.

Ghaneemah: غنيمه

Spoils; booty; loot; prey: something acquired without labour..

Gohar: گوهر

(Persian): Diamond; precious stone.

Gul-e-ranaa: گل رعنا

(Persian): A beautiful delicate scented rose.

Gulshan: گلشن

(Persian): A rose or flower garden.

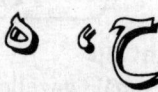

Haabeel: هابيل

Name of the son of Hazrat Aadam (Adam)عليه السلام.

Haadi: هادى

A director; a leader; a guide.

Haafizh: حافظ

(Haafiz): A guardian; a governor; preserver; protector; the preserver of all things; God; having a good memory; one who knows the whole Quran by heart; the poetical name of celebrated poet of Persian(Muhammad Shamsuddin Shiraazi).

Haajib: حاجب

Doorkeeper; chamberlain;eyebrow.

Haami: حامي

A protector; a patron; helper; supporter; defender.

Haamid: حامد

One who praises.

Haani:هاني

Pleasant; name of a Sahabi who participated in the battle of Badr.

Haaris: حارس

A door keeper; a chamberlain; a farmer.

Ḥaarith: حارث

(Haaris): Farmer; name of a famous Sahabi (RA).

Ḥaarithah: حارثه

(Haarisah): Name of a Sahabi who participated in the battle of Badr

Haaroon: هارون

Name of the prophet of Allah; his English equivalent is Aaron.

Ḥaashid: حاشد

One who gathers the people together; the Name of the son of Imaam Bukhaari(RA), A great Muhaddith.

Haashim: هاشم

A crusher; breaker.

Ḥaashir: حاشر

An assembler.

Haashimi: هاشمى

A person who belongs to an Arab tribe, Bani Hashim.

Ḥaatib: حاطب

A person who collects wood; name of a Sahabi who participated in the battle of Badr; He was the messenger of the Holy prophet (peace be upon him) to the ruler of Egypt.

Ḥaazim: حازم

Precautious; Name of a Sahabi.

Habib: حبيب

Lover; beloved.

Hafeezh: حفيظ

(Hafeez): Guardian , Protector, an attribute applied to Allah . Names: Abdul Hafeez .

Hafs: حفص

Name of a well known Quari.

Haidar: حيدر

A blood thirsty lion; the title of Hazrat Ali(RA).

Hajjaaj: حجاج

One who prevails in the argument; Name of famous ruler of Iraq known as Hajjaaj ibn Yousof

Hakam: حكم

An umpire; a mediator; an arbitrator; name of a caliph of Arab. An attribute applied to Allah.

Hakeem: حكيم

Wise; a sage; a philosopher; a physician; a doctor. An attribute applied to Allah.

Haleef: حليف

Ally; comrade; sworn; friend.

Haleem: حليم

A patient man; an attribute of Allah Almighty. Names: AbdulHaleem; Muhammad Haleem.

Hamd: حمد

Praise; admiration.

Hamdan: حمدان

The one who praises (Allah).

Hameed: حميد

> Praise worthy; He who is the only one to be praised and glorified and thanked by all creatures. Name:Abdul Hameed; Muhammad Hameed.

Hameem: حميم

> Friend; hot water.

Hammaad: حمّاد

> A person who praises, commends or thanks Allah most.

Hammam: همّام

> Name of a great scholar of Hadith who is known as Hammam bin Munabih.

Hamnah: حمنه

> Name of a Sahabiyyah, who is known as Hamnah bint Jahsh and she was a sister of Hazrat Zainab (RA).

Hamood: حمود

> A person who praises and thanks Allah.

Hamzah: حمزه

> Lion; name of the beloved uncle of the Holy Prophet ﴾ﷺ﴿ whose appelation was Asadullah and asadu-Rasool meaning: 'Lion of Allah' and 'Lion of the Holy prophet ﴾ﷺ﴿.

Haneef: حنيف

> Upright; True; true believer.

Hannan: حنان

> Allah's attribute;meaning: Most Merciful and Most forgiving. Name Abdul Hannan.

Hanzhalah:حنظله

(Hanzalah): The name of a tree; the name of a Sahabi who was one of the scribes of the Holy Prophet (Peace be upon him).

Haq: حق

(Haque) The Truth; He whose existence has no change; Allah's attribute. Name: Abdul-Haque.

Haraam: حرام

Name of a Sahabi who participated in the battle of Badr.

Hareef: حريف

Opponent.

Hareem: حريم

A respectable.

Harmalah: حرمله

A plant; Name of a famous Sahabi(RA).

Haseeb: حسيب

A person with a noble lineage or family back ground; an attribte of Allah ; Names:Abdul Haseeb, Muhammad Haseeb, Haseeb Ahmed .

Haseen:حسَين

Beautiful; smart.

Hashmat: حشمت

Dignity;glory.

Hasan: حَسن

Good; Name of the grand son of the Holy prophet peace be upon him i.e.. the son of Hazrat Fatimah and Hazrat Ali.

Hassaan: حسان

Name of a distinguished Sahabi(RA) known as the poet of the prophet peace be upon him.

Haushab: حوشب

Name of son of Imam Muslim (RA), a great Muhaddith.

Hayaat : حيات

Life.

Hayy: حي

Ever alive, an attribute applied exclusively to Allah . Name: Abdul-Hayy.

Hayyaan: حيان

Alive; Name of a Raavi, who narrates the Sayings of the prophet peace be upon him.

Hibah: هبه

Grant; donation; present.

Hibbaan: حبان

Name of a Scholar of Hadith.

Hidayat: هدايت

Instruction; guidance; righteousness.

Hilaal: هلال

Crescent; Name of a Sahabi who participated in the batle of Badr .

Himaayat: حمايت

Protection; guardianship; patronage; support; defense; countenance.

Hishaam: هشام

Name of a distinguished Sahabi(RA) known for

his fatwas and narration of ahadith.

Hood: هود

   Name of a prophet of Almighty Allah.

Hubab: حباب

   Name of a Sahabi who participated in the battle
of Badr.

Hubail: هبيل

   Name of a Sahabi who participated in the battle
of Badr.

Hubaish: حبيش

   Name of a Tabi'i.

Hud: هود

   Name of prophet of Allah Almighty.

Hudhaifah: حذيفه

   (Huzaifah): Name of a distinguished Sahabi(RA)
known as the confident of the prophet peace be
upon him.

Hujjat: حُجت

   Argument; proof; reason; discussion.

Humaam: همام

   A respectable leader.

Humaid: حميد

   Praised; Name of many scholars of Hadith.

Humail: هميل

   Name of a Sahabi.

Humayoon: همايون

   (Persian) Name of a Mugul king of India.

Ḥuraith: حريث

A little farmer; Name of a Sahabi who participated in the battle of Badr.

Ḥurmat: حرمت

Dignity; honor; reverence; reputation; chastity; esteem.

Ḥurrah: حره

Liberal; free.

Ḥusaam: حُسام

Sword; a good combination: Husaam uddeen.

Ḥuṣain: حُصين

Name of a Sahabi who participated in the battle of Badr.

Ḥusain: حُسين

Grand son of the Holy prophet peace be upon him i.e.. the son of Hazrat Fatimah and Hazrat Ali (RA).

Ḥuzaifah: حذيفه

(Hudhaifah): Name of a distinguished Sahabi(RA) known as the confident of the prophet peace be upon him.

Female Names

Haadiyah: هادیه
A director; a leader; a guide.

Haafizah: حافظه
Having a good memory; one who knows the whole Quran by heart.

Haajirah: هاجره
The wife of Hazrat Ibrahim, peace be upon him.

Haalah: هاله
A crescent-shaped ear-ring; name of the sister of Hazrat Khadijatulkubraa (RA).

Haamidah: حامده
One who praises.

Haarisah: حارسة
Guard; protector.

Haarithah: حارثه
Name of a Sahabi who participated in the battle of Badr .

Habeebah: حبیبه
Beloved.

Hadiqah: حدیقه
Garden.

Hafeezhah: حنیظه
(Hafeezah): Guardian , Protector.

Hafṣah: حفصه
.
> The wife of the Holy prophet, peace be upon him; and Ummulmoominin, mother of the believers; and the daughter of Hazrat Umar(RA).

Hakeemah: حكيمه
.
> A sage; philosopher; a physician; a doctor.

Haleemah: حليمه
.
> (Halimah)A patient woman; A wet nurse of the Holy prophet peace be upon him.

Hameedah: حميده
.
> Praise worthy.

Hamraa': حمرآء
.
> Red colored female.

Hanfaa': حنفآء
.
> The wife of Hazrat Ismail (Ishmael) ,peace be upon him.

Hani: هانى
> Pleasant.

Hanifa: حنيفه
.
> Upright; True; true believer.

Hannah: حنّه
.
> The mother of Hazrat Maryam(Mary); and the wife of Imran who is mentioned in the Holy Quran.

Haola: حولاء
> Name of a Sahabiah; she was also a jurist and scholar of Islamic law.

Harithah: حارثه
    Name of a Sahabi(RA).

Haseenah: حسينه
    Pretty girl.

Hasnaa': حسنآء
    pretty woman.

Hawwaa': حوّاء
    One who rejects falsehood and follows the truth; the wife of Hazrat Aadam (Peace be upon him).

Hibbah: حبّ
    Beloved.

Hinaa': حنا
    The Indian privet; a shrub, the leaves of which are used for dyeing the hands, feet and hair.

Hind: هند
    Name of Ummulmoomineen, the wife of the prophet peace be upon him, who is known also as Umme Salamah(RA).

Hindah: هنده
    Name of wife of AbuSufyaan, a Sahabi of the Holy prophet peace be upon him.

Hoor: حور
    A virgin of Paradise; a black eyed nymph; a celestial bride promised to all good Muslims in the hear after.

Huda : هُدى

Guidance towards the right direction; the right path; instruction.

Hujaimah: هُجيمه

Name of a Sahabiah known as Umm-Darda'(RA).

Huma: هما

(Persian word) Name of an emaginary bird.

Humairaa': حُميرآء

Red colored girl; Name of Ummulmoominin Hazrat Aaishah (RA).

Husnaa: حُسنى

Most pious; most beautiful; most precious.

Ibrahim : ابراهيم

Name of the well-known prophet of Allah; and name of Hazrat Muhammad's (peace be upon him) son.

Idrees: ادريس

Name of a well-known Messenger of Allah.

Iftikhaar: افتخار

To be proud of.

Ihsaan: احسان

Doing good; beneficence; kindness; favour.

Ihtishaam: احتشام

Having many followers or dependents; magnificence.

Ihtiraam: احترام

Honour; veneration; treating with respect; holding in veneration; act of honoring; reverence.

Ikhlaas: اخلاص

Sincerity; purity; love; tenderness; pure friendship; great affection; selfless adoration or worship.

Ikraam: اکرام

Honoring; treating with attention; and ceremony; esteem; veneration; respect; deference; kindness; favour.

Iltifaat: التفات

Regard; attention; kindness; courtesy; consideration; friendship; inclination.

Ilyas: الياس

Name of a prophet of Allah Almighty; and name of a great scholar and saint who was the founder of Tablighi Jamaat.

'Imaad: عماد

Foundation; pillar.

Imam: امام

Spritual or religious leader (of Muslims).

'Imran: عمران

Name of a Sahabi who took part in the battle of Badr;and known as Imran ibn Husain(RA).

Imtiyaaz: امتياز

Discernment; pre-eminence; distinction; preference.

Inaam: انعام

A present ; gift; prize; gratuity; reward; favour; grant.

'Inayat: عنايت

Favour; bounty; kindness; support; care; gift; present.

Intikhaab: انتخاب

Selection; to choose.

Intezaar: انتظار

To wait.

Iqbaal: اقبال

Prosperity; good fortune; luck; success; felicity; name of the great philosopher-poet of India-Pakistan subcontinent who was the first to conceive the idea of a separate home-land(Pakistan) for Muslims of united India.

Iqtidaar: اقتدار

Power; authority; influence; eminence; dignity; rank.

'Irfaan: عرفان

Recognition; knowledge; discernment; science; wisdom.

Irshaad: ارشاد

Instruction; command; behest; order; direction; will; pleasure.

'Isa: عیسی

('Isa) Name of a prophet of Allah Almighty; Its English equivalent is Jesus.

Ieethaar: ایثار

(Isaar): Sacrifice; selflessness.

Ishaq: اسحاق

Name of a prophet of Allah Almighty; Its English equivalent is Isaac.

'Ishrat: عشرت

Pleasure; enjoyment; delight; mirth; society; pleasant and familiar conversation.

Ishtiyaaq: اشتیاق

Longing; cravnig; yearning; desire; liking; fondness; eagerness; strong inclination.

Iskandar: اسکندر

Alexender

Islaam: اسلام

(Lit. Submission to Allah) the Muslim's religion; Islam.

Ismaa'eel: اسماعیل

> (Ismail) Name of a prophet of Allah, son of
> Hazrat Ibrahim (علیهما السلام) It is said that this
> name is composed of two words , *Ism'* means:
> *listen1!* and *eel* means: *Allah* in the *Syriac* lan-
> guage.In other words " Hear and grant my
> prayers, O Allah!" ; Its English equivalent is
> Ishmael.

Israa'eel: اسرائیل

> (Lit. One chosen by God) a servant of God;
> the surname of Yaqoob (Jacob), علیه اسلام Israel.

'Itbaan: عتبان

> Name of a Sahabi who took part in the battle
> of Badr.

Iyaas: اباس

> Name of a Sahabi who took part in the battle
> of Badr.

'Iyaaz: عیاض

> Name of a Sahabi who took part in the battle
> of Badr.

Izzat: عزّت

> Honor; esteem; integrity.

Female Names

'Iffat: عفت

Purity; chastity; modesty; decency; virtue; abstinence; continence.

'Ishrat: عشرت

Pleasure; enjoyment; delight; mirth; society; pleasant and familiar conversation.

'Ismat: عصمت

Name of a Sahabi who took part in the battle of Badr.

'Izzat: عزت

Honor; esteem; integrity.

J

Jaabir: جابر

One who repairs the loss; Name of a Sahabi who participated in the battle of Badr .

Jaan: جان

(Persian): Soul; life.

Jabalah: جبله

Name of a Sahabi who participated in the battle of Badr .

Jabbaar: جبار

(Arabic) Mighty; One who had the ascendancy; king; One who commiserates the bereaved, an attribute of Allah; Name Abdul Jabbaar.

Jabr: جبر

Name of a Sahabi who participated in the battle of Badr.

Ja'far: جعفر

Name of a famous Sahabi(RA).

Jahangeer: جهانگیر

(Persian): Name of a Mogul king.

Jahm: جهم

Name of a Sahabi .

Jalaal: جلال

Grandeur;greatness; eminence; glory; majesty.

Jaleel: جلیل

Great; glorious; illustrious; dignified. An attribute of Allah.

Jalees: جليس

A companion; chum; a fast friend; comrade.

Jamaal: جمال

Beauty; elegance ; comeliness ; of good looks and character.

Jameel: جميل

Handsome; Physically and morally attractive; name of a Sahabi , the companion of the prophet (peace be upon him).

Jandarah: جندره

Name of a Sahabi .

Jaraah: جراح

Name of a Sahabi .

Jareer: جرير

Name of a distinguished Sahabi(RA).

Jarraah: جرّاح

Name of a *Taab'i*; and a *Raavi*.

Jaarood: جارود

Name of a distinguished Sahabi (RA).

Jaseem: جسيم

Corpulent; bulky.

Jawaad: جواد

Swift horse; beneficent; bountiful.

Jawwaad: جوّاد

Liberal; Most beneficent; bountiful; most generous. It is also an attribute of Allah; suitabl name: Abdul Jawwad.

Jiyaad: جياد

(pl. of jayyid) Very good; Name of a mountain in Makkah Mukarramah.

Johar: جوهر

A gem; a jewel; a pearl; atom ;skill; knowledge; secret; nature; matter; substance; essence; acid; virtue; worth; merit.

Jubair: جبير

Name of a Sahabi who participated in the battle of Badr .

Juhaim: جُهيم

Name of a Sahabi .

Ju'ail: جُعيل

Name of a Sahabi .

Jumaanah: جُمانه

Name of a Sahabi .

Jummal: جُمّل

A thick rope; a rope with which a boat is tied to the shore.

Junaid: جُنيد

Small section of an army; Name of a Sahabi; Name of a great Tabi'i and great saint known as Junaid Baghdadi..

Jundub: جُندب

Name of a Sahabi .

Juthaamah: جُثامه

(Jusamah) Name of a Sahabi; and also Name of a Sahabiyyah(RA).

Jaudaan: جردان

Name of a Sahabi .

Female Names

Jaan: جان
> (Persian) Soul; life.

Jabeen: جبين
> The forehead.

Jahan Ara: جهان آرا
> (Persian) One who adorns the world.

Jaleelah: جليله
> Great; glorious; illustrious; dignified.

Jamaal: جمال
> Beauty; elegance ; comeliness ; of good looks
> and character.

Jameelah: جميله
> Physically and morally attractive; good look-
> ing; beautiful; pretty girl.

Jariyah: جاريه
> A girl; a slave- girl.

Juwariah: جويريه
> A small girl; Name of an Ummulmoomineen,
> the wife of the Holy Prophet peace be upon
> him.

Jauhar: جوهر
> A gem; a jewel; a pearl; atom ;skill; knowl-
> edge; secret; nature; matter; substance; es-
> sence; acid; virtue; worth; merit.

Johi: جوہی
> (Urdu) Jasmine.

Jumaanah: جُمانہ
> Name of a Sahabi .

Jumaim'ah: جُميمہ
> Name of a Sahabiyyah(RA).

Jumainah: جُمينہ
> Name of a Sahabiyyah(RA).

Ka'b: كعب

> (Kaab)Knot (of cane); joint; ankle; anklebone; heel(of the foot; of a shoe) ferrule; die; cube; high rank; glory; Name of a Sahabi who took part in the battle of Badr.

Kaamil: كامل

> Perfect; complete; accomplished; learned.

Kaashif: كاشف

> Discoverer; detective; revealer; explorer.

Kaazhim: كاظم

> (Kaazim): A person who suppresses his anger.

Kabeer: كبير

> Immense; great; senior; Allah's attribute.

Kafeel: كفيل

> A surety; a security; guarantee .

Kaif: كيف

> A state of joy.

Kaisaan: كيسان

> Wise; Name of a distinguished Sahabi(RA).

Kaleem: كليم

> A speaker; an interlocutor.

Kalimullah: كليم الله

> One who has conversation with Allah; Moses.

Kamaal: كمال

Perfection; completion; excellence; something wonderful; miracle.

Karaamat: كرامت

Name of a distinguished Sahabi(RA).

Kareem: كريم

Bountiful; generous; magnificent; gracious; merciful; modest; an attribute of Allah Almighty.

Karraar: كرّار

Attacking violently again and again; impetuous.

Katheer: كثير

(Kaseer): Name of a distinguished Sahabi (RA).

Kaukab: كوكب

A star.

Kauthar: كوثر

(Kosar) Name of a fountain in Jannah,the paradise.

Khaadim: خادم

Servant; an attendant.

Khaalid: خالد

Permanent; Name of a Sahabi who participated in the battle of Badr; also name of a Sahabi known as Khaalid ibn waleed, famous as a great general of Muslims who conquered a number of countries.

Khaarijah: خارجه

Name of a Sahabi who participated in the battle of Badr.

Khabbaab: خباب

Name of a Sahabi who participated in the battle of Badr.

Khabeer: خبير

:Informer, Allah's attribute; One who knows of every thing . Name: Abdul Khabeer .

Khafiz: خانض

(Khafid) He who diminishes or decreases . Name: Abdul Khaafiz.

Khair: خير

adj. Good; best; well; safe; adv. Very well ; Goodness; welfare; happiness; health.

Khalaf: خلف

A successor; an heir; a favorite son; posterity; descendants; adj. Dutiful.

Khaleed: خليد

Name of a Sahabi (RA).

Khaleel: خليل

Friend; the title of Hazrat Ibrahim, the prophet of Allah Almighty.

Khaleeq: خليق

Of good disposition; kind; affable; benign; civil; polite; obliging; courteous; well disposed.

Khallaad: خلّاد

Name of a Sahabi who participated in the battle of Badr .

Khateeb: خطيب

A preacher; A public speaker or orator.

Khawly: خولي

Name of a Sahabi who participated in the battle of Badr .

Khawwaath: خوّات

(Khawwas): Name of a Sahabi who participated in the battle of Badr .

Khidaash: خداش

Name of a Sahabi who participated in the battle of Badr .

Khirash: خِراش

Name of a Sahabi who participated in the battle of Badr .

Khooshbakht: خوشبخت

Of good fortune.

Khursheed: خورشید

(Persian) The sun.

Khubaib: خُبیب

Name of a Sahabi who participated in the battle of Badr .

Khulaidah: خُلیده

Name of a Sahabi who participated in the battle of Badr .

Khulaifah: خُلیفه

Name of a Sahabi who participated in the battle of Badr .

Khunais: خُنیس

Name of a Sahabi who participated in the battle of Badr .

Khuraim: خُرَيم

    Name of a Sahabi who participated in the battle of Badr .

Kifayat: كفايت

    Enough; abundance; profit; ability; prudence; plenty; surplus; economy; thrift; sufficiency.

Kishwar: كشور

    (Persian): A country; a territory; climate; region.

Kulthum: كلثوم

    Name of a Sahabi(RA).

Kuraib: كُرَيب

    Name of a distinguished Sahabi(RA).

Female Names

Kaamilah: كامله

Complete; perfect.

Kaashifah: كاشفه

Discoverer; detective; revealer; explorer.

Kabeerah: كبيره

Immense; great; senior; Name of a Sahabiyah.

Kabshah: كبشه

A goat; Name of a Sahabiyyah(RA).

Kaif: كيف

A state of joy.

Kaleemah: كليمه

A speaker; an interlocutor; Name of a Saha-biyyah.

Kaneezah: كنيزه

Firm;(of flesh); sturdy (of body).

Kanzah: كنزه

Treasure.

Kareemah: كريمه

Bountiful; generous; magnificent; gracious; merciful.

Kaukab: كوكب

A star.

Kauthar: كوثر

(Kosar) :Much; abundant; large; quantity; a river in Paradise.

Kehkashan: كهكشان

(Persian): The milky way; galaxy.

Khaalidah: خالد

Permanent; durable ; one who does not grow weak even in old age.

Khaareejah: خارجه

Name of a Sahabi who participated in the battle of Badr .

Khadijah: خديجه

Name of Ummulmoomineen Hazrat Khadijah who was the first wife of the Holy Prophet peace be upon him.

Khairah: خيره

adj. Good; best; well; safe; adv. Very well. Goodness; welfare; happiness; health.

Khaleesah: خليسه

Name of a Sahabiyyah(RA).

Khansaa': خنساء

Name of a Sahabiyyah(RA).

Kharqa': خرقآء

Name of a Sahabiyyah(RA).

Khaulah: خوله

Name of a Sahabiyyah(RA).

Khidrah: خضره

(Khizrah): Name of a Sahabiyyah(RA).

Khudamah: خدامه

Name of a Sahabiyyah(RA).

Kholah: خوله
> Name of a Sahabiyyah(RA).

Khursheed: خورشید
> (Persian) The sun.

Khooshbakht: خوش بخت
> Of good fortune.

Khudrah: خُضره
> (Khuzrah): Name of a Sahabiyyah(RA).

Khulaidah: خلیده
> Name of a Sahabi who participated in the
> battle of Badr; and name of a Sahabiyyah.

Khuwailah: خویله
> Name of a women

Khuzaimah: خُزیمه
> Name of a Sahabi Sahabiyyah(RA).

Kishwar: کشور
> (Persian) A country; a territory; climate; re-
> gion.

Kowaisah: کویسه
> Name of a Sahabiyyah.

Kubraa: کبری
> Bigger.

Kulthoom: کلثوم
> (Kulsoom): Name of a Sahabiyyah (RA).

Laaiq: لائق
> Skillful; eligible. capable of; able.

Labeeb: لبیب
> Intelligent; brilliant.

Labeed: لبید
> Intelligent; brilliant. Name of a Sahabi(R.A).

La'eeq: لئیق
> Skillful; subtle; eligible. capable of; able.

Lateef: لطیف
> Delicious; delicate; subtle agreeable; fine; courteous; elegant; benevolent; also an attribute applied to Allah Almighty.

Liyaqat: لیاقت
> Worth; ability; fitness; capability; capacity; aptitude; merit; skill.

Loot: لوط
> (Lut) Name of a prophet of Allah.

Luqmaan: لقمان
> Name of a well known person as a sage; philosopher.

Lutf: لطف
> Enjoyment; entertainment; bounty. Name: Lutfullah.

Female Names

Labeebah: لبيبه

A wise woman; Name of a Sahabiyyah.

Lailaa: ليلى

Name of a Sahabiyyah.

Latifah: لطيفه

Delicious; delicate; subtle; agreeable; fine; courteous; elegant; benevolent.

Layyah: ليّه

Name of a Sahabiyyah.

Leena: لينا

Name of a Sahabiyyah.

Lubabah: لبابه

Name of a Sahabiyyah.

Lubnaa: لبنى

Name of a Sahabiyyah.

Maahir: ماهر
Skillful; able; experienced.

Maajid: ماجد
Glorious; honorable; generous; splendid; Allah's attribute. Name: AbdulMajid.

Maalik: مالك
Master; lord; an attribute applied to Allah Almighty; Name of a Sahabi who took part in the battle of Badr ; Name of a great jurist and scholar of Hadith.

Maani': مانع
One who Prevents.

Ma'bad: معبد
Name of a Sahabi who took part in the battle of Badr.

Madani: مدنى
Related to Madina.

Madhat: مدحت
Praise; eulogy.

Mahboob: محبوب
Beloved.

Mahfoozh: محفوظ

(Mahfooz): Secured; protected; safe.

Maheen: مهين

Fine; thin; not coarse; feeble.

Mahja': مهجع

Name of a Sahabi who participated in the battle of Badr.

Mahmood: محمود

Praised; praiseworthy; laudable; worthy.

Maimoon: ميمون

Fortunate; auspicious; prosperous.

Majeed: مجيد

Glorious; Immense; enormous; noble; exalted; an attribute of Allah Almighty. Names: Abdul Majeed; Muhammad Majeed.

Makhdoom: مخدوم

Served; waited on.

Makki: مكى

Related to Makkat ul Mukarramah.

Ma'mar: معمر

Name of a Sahabi who participated in the battle of Badr.

Mamoon: مامون

Secured; Name of a caliph of Islam.

Ma'moor: معمور

Inhabited; populated; full; relate; abundant;

colonized; ample; happy; delightful; prosperous; flourishing; in good condition.

Ma'n: معن
Name of a Sahabi who took part in the battle of Badr.

Mannaan: منّان
A great benefactor; an attribute applied to Allah Almighty. Name: Abdul Mannan.

Mansoor: منصور
Aided; protected; defended; victorious; conquering; triumphant.

Manzhar: منظر
(Manzar): A Sight; landscape; scene.

Manzhoor: منظور
(Manzoor): Agreed; approved; accepted.

Maqbool: مقبول
Agreed; approved; accepted.

Ma'qil: معقل
Name of a Sahabi who took part in the battle of Badr.

Maqsood: مقصود
Intended; proposed. object; aim; view.

Marghoob: مرغوب
Desirable; amiable; beautiful; lovely; pleasant; excellent; agreeable.

Ma'roof: معروف

well-known; famous; popular; illustrious; good deed.

Marthad: مرثد

(Marsad): Name of a Sahabi(RA).

Marwaan: مروان

Name of a ruler in early Islamic history.

Marzooq: مرزوق

Recipient of sustenance by Allah; Name of a Sahabi(RA).

Mashhood: مشهود

Attested; proved; evidenced; clear; manifest; present.

Mashkoor: مشكور

Praised; thanked; laudable; agreeable.

Ma'sood: مسعود

Blessed; Name of a Sahabi who took part in the battle of Badr.

Ma'soom: معصوم

Defennded; preserved; innocent; simple; guiltless; infant.

Masroor: مسرور

Glad; pleased; cheerful; delighted; exalting.

Mateen: متين

Firmed; constant; solid; a person who has

depth in his thoughts.

Matloob: مطلوب

Aim; goal; destination; desire.

Mazhar: مظهر

A place of spectacle; manifestation.

Mehtaab: مهتاب

(Persian): The moon.

Me'maar: معمار

(Urdu): A builder.

Me'raaj: معراج

A ladder; anything by which one ascends; ascension; ascension of the Holy Prophet to Heaven.

Midlaj: مدلج

Name of a Sahabi who took part in the battle of Badr.

Miftaah: مفتاح

A key.

Minhaaj: منهاج

Highway or road.

Miqdaad: مقداد

Name of a Sahabi who took part in the battle of Badr.

Mirsab: مرسب

Prudent; wise; name of the sword of the Holy

prophet ﴾ﷺ﴿.

Misbaah: مصباح

A lamp ; a lamp light; lantern; a morning.

Miskeen: مسكين

Poor; miserable; humble; indigent; meek.

Mistah: مسطح

Name of a Sahabi who took part in the battle of Badr.

Mansoor: منصور

Aided; protected; defended; victorious; conquering.

Moosa: موسى

Name of a prophet of Allah, his equivalent in English is Moses.

Mu'aadh: معاذ

(Muaaz): Name of a great Sahabi who participated in the battle of Badr and who was sent as a governor of Yaman in the days of the prophet peace be upon him.

Mu'awiyah: معاويه

Name of a famous Sahabi who was the caliph after Hazrat Ali(RA); and he was one of the scribes of the Holy Prophet ﴾ﷺ﴿.

Mua'wwadh: مُعَوَّذ

(Muawwaz): Name of a Sahabi who participated in the battle of Badr.

Muawwidh: مُعَوِّذ

(Muawwiz): Name of a Sahabi(RA) who participated in the battle of Badr and killed Abu Jahl.

Mua'zhzham: معظم

(Muazzam): A big; great; distinguished; graceful; honorable.

Mubaarak: مبارك
Auspicious; blessed; august; sacred; holy; happy; fortunate.

Mubash'shir: مبشر
A bearer of glad tidings or good news; an announcer(of good news); Name of a Sahabi who took part in the battle of Badr.

Muballigh: مبلغ
A preacher of Islam; a person who propagates Islam.

Mubassir: مبصر

Analyst; name of a Sahabi who participated in the battle of Badr.

Mubeen: مبين

One who makes something clear.

Mudabbir: مدبر
Skilled in devising; prudent; ingenious; governing.

Muddath'thir: مدَّثر

A title of the Holy prophet peace be upon him.

Mudhakkir: مذكر

(Muzakkir): Reminding.

Mu'eed: معيد

The Restorer; He who restores all beings; Name: Abdul-Mueed.

Mu'eedh: مُعيذ

(Mu'eez): A person who gives shelter.

Mu'een: معين

Helper; Assistant

Mufakkir: مفكر

Mediator; considerate; a thinker.

Mufallah: مفلح

A person who got prosperity or betterment.

Mufazzal: مفضّل

(Mufaddal): Preferable; preferred.

Mufeed: مُفيض

(Mufeez) He who pours forth; fills; overflows ; pours or pours out.

Muflih: مفلح

Prosperous.

Mufti: مفتى

Jurist; scholar of Islamic law.

Mughni: مغنى

Sufficient.

Muhaafizh: محافظ

(Muhaafiz) Guard.

Muhaimin: مُهيمن

One who provides sanctuary from any hazard
of danger, one who protects; one who is merciful; an attribute of Allah Almighty. Name: Abdul Muhaimih.

Muhaajir: مهاجر

A person who migrates ; name of a Sahabi

Muhammad: محمّد

The name of the last prophet of Almighty Allah ﴿ ﷺ ﴾.

Muhdi: مهدى

He who givs present.

Muheet: محيط

Surrounding; comprehensive.

Muhib: محب

Lover; friend.

Muhriz: محرز

Name of a Sahabi who took part in the battle
of Badr.

Muhsin: محسن
  A benefactor; a patron.

Muhtashim: محتشم
  Great; powerful; attended by many followers or dependents; having many followers.

Muhyee: مُحيي
  One who gives and sustains life reviver one of the attributes of Almighty Allah. Name: Muhiyyuddeen.

Mu'izz: معز
  (Muizz) One who bestows honor i.e.. Allah Almighty. Name: AbdulMu'izz.

Mujaddid: مجدد
  Renovator.

Mujahid: مجاهد
  A warrior in the defense of true faith;

Mujazzir: مجزّر
  Name of a Sahabi who took part in the battle of Badr.

Mujeeb: مجيب
  One who answers; one who accepts or grants something; Allah's attribute. Name; AbdulMujeeb; Mujeeb Ahmed.

Mujtabaa: مجتبى
  Chosen; selected; a title of the holy prophet, peace be upon him.

Mukarram: مكرم

Respected, Honorable.

Mukhtaar: مختار

Selected; independent;authorized; empowered.

Mulail: مُليل

Name of a Sahabi who participated in the battle of Badr.

Mumin: مومن

The believer; one who embraced Islam by heart.

Mumtaaz: ممتاز

Distinguished; exalted; illustrious; eminent.

Munaaf: مناف·

Name of a Sahabi who took part in the battle of Badr.

Munawwar:منور

Brilliant; illuminated; enlightened; splendid.

Muneeb: منيب

One who turns to Allah;

Muneer: منير

Brilliant; shining; illuminated; enlightened; splendid.

Mun'im: منعم

Generous; bountiful; benefactor; Name: Ab-dulMun'im.

Munqaad: منقاد
Obedient.

Muntaqim: منتقم
The Avenger; He who punishes wrongdoers; One who takes revenge. Name : Abdul Muntaquim.

Muntasir: منتصر
Title of a caliph of Islam.

Mundhir: منذر
(Munzir): Warner, Name of a Sahabi who participated in the battle of Badr.

Muqaddas: مقدس
Holy; distinguished.

Muqbil: مقبل
Coming; next, attentive,

Muqeet : مقيت
The Maintainer; He who sustains. Name: Abdul-Muqeet.

Muqsit: مقسط
Just; impartial; who does justice. Name: Abdul-Muqsit.

Muqtasid: مقتصد
One who adopts a middle course; acts as a mediator.

Muqutadir: مقتدر
Powerful; mighty; Allah's attribute. Name: Ab-

dul-Muqutadir.

Muraad: مراد
A wish; desire; intended.

Murabbi: مربی
A guardian; patron; protector; supporter; head; fostered.

Murarah: مراره
Name of a Sahabi who participated in the battle of Badr.

Mursal: مرسل

A messenger; a prophet; an apostle; an ambassador. adj. sent to another with a message.

Murshid: مرشد
An instructor; a guide; a spiritual teacher; a monitor; the head of a religious order; a director.

Murtaad: مُرتاض
(Murtaaz): Disciplined; one who endeavours in worshipping Almighty Allah and in suppressing the desires of the *nafs* or self.

Murtadaa: مرتضی
(Murtazaa) Chosen; selected; agreeable; a title of Hazrat Ali.

Mus'ab: مصعب
Name of a Sahabi who particepated in the battle of Badr.

Musaddiq: مصدق

Verifier; one who believes another; one who gives Sadaquah, charity .

Maṣarrat: مسرت

Happiness; pleasure.

Muṣawwir: مصور

He who designs all things. Name: Abdul Musawwir.

Musharraf: مشرف

Exalted; ennobled; honored;

Musheer: مشير

A counselor; a senator; an adviser; secretary.

Mushfiq: مشفق

kind; dear; affectionate; showing favour; condoling.

Mushtaaq: مشتاق

Desirous; longing; ardent; fond; wishful; wishing.

Muṣlih: مصلح

Reformer, Name of a great saint known as Muslihuddin Shirazi.

Muslim: مسلم

One who submits to Allah, A believer in one God, Allah, and His prophets.

Musta'een: مُستعين

Praying for help; soliciting aid.

Muṣṭafaa : مصطنى
Chosen; selected; a title of the who Holy Prophet peace be upon him.

Mustafeed: مستنيد
Profiting; gaining; acquiring.

Mustafeed: مستفيض
(Mustafeez):Pofittining; one who is desirous of gaining. Name: Mustafeezur-Rahmaan.

Mustajaab: مستجاب
Heard; granted; given ear to; acceptable; agreeable. One whose prayers are accepted by Allah.

Mustaneer: مستنير
Bright; brilliant; shining.

Mustaqeem: مستقيم
Right; straight; erect; direct; faithful.

Mustataab: مُستطاب
Happy; glad; pleased.

Mustazhir: مستظهر
(Mustaz, hir) Praying for help; soliciting aid.

Musthasan: مستحسن
Better; Suitable.

Mutahhir: مطهّر
That which purifies.

Mutakabbir: متكبر

The Majestic; He who shows His greatness in all things and in all ways. Name: Abdul Mutakabbir.

Mu'tasim: معتصم
Name of a caliph of Islam.

Mu'attib: معتّب
Name of a Sahabi who participated in the battle of Badr.

Mutawassit: متوسط
Moderate.

Mutee': مطيع
Obedient.

Mutayyib: مطيّب
Giving fragrance; perfuming.

Muttaqi: متقى
God fearing; pious.

Muzhaffar: مظفر

(Muzaffar): Victorious, successful; rendered victorious and aided by Allah.

Muzzammil: مزّمل
A title of the Holy Prophet, peace be upon him.

Muzhir: مُظهِر

(Muz,,hir) Name of a Sahabi who participated in the battle of Badr.

Female Names

Maahirah: ماهرة
Skillful; able; experienced.

Maajidah: ماجده
Glorious; honorable; generous; splendid.

Maalikah: مالكه
Mistress.

Maariya: ماريه
A lady with fair complexion; The bondmaid of the Holy Prophet ﷺ

Madhat: مدحت
Praise.

Mahfoozah: محفوظه
(Mahfoozhah) Secured; protected; safe.

Mahmoodah: محموده
Praiseworthy; praised; elegant.

Maimoona: ميمونه
(Maimoonah) Fortunate; auspicious; prosperous. Name of an Ummulmoomineen, the wife of the Holy prophet peace be upon him.

Majeedah: مجيده
Glorious; honorable; generous; splendid.

Maknoonah: مكنونه
Hidden; concealed.

Maleekah:مَلِیکه
Name of a Sahabiyyah (RA).

Maleehah: ملیحه
Salty; nut brown; of dark brown color, agreeable; sweet; charming; beautiful; graceful.

Malikah: مَلِکه
A queen.

Marjanah:مرجانه
A precious stone, Name of a Sahabiyyah (RA).

Maryam: مریم
Name of the mother of Hadrat 'eesaa (Jesus) peace be upon him; its equivalent in English is Mary.

Mashhoodah: مشهوده
Attested; proved; evidence; clear; manifest; present.

Ma'soomah: معصومه
Innocent; protected.

Mas'uoodah: مسعوده
Present; manifest.

Mateenah: متینه
Firmed; constant; solid; a woman who has depth in his thoughts.

Mehtaab: مهتاب
The moon.

Miskeenah: مسكينه

Humble.

Mansoorah: منصوره

Aided; protected; defended; victorious; conquering; triumphant; succored.

Muaazah: مُعاذة

(Muadhah) Name of a Sahabiyyah (RA).

Mubaarakah: مباركه

Auspicious; blessed; august; sacred; holy; happy; fortunate.

Mubash'shirah: مبشره

A bearer of glad tidings or good news.

Mubassirah: مبصره

An analyst; critic..

Mubeenah: مبينه

A woman who makes something clear.

Mu'eenah: معينه

An assistant; a helper; an aiding.

Mu'eerah: مُعيره

A girl who gives a borrowing.

Mugheethah: مغيثه

She who helps, rescues, relieves.

Muhsinah: محسنة

A benefactor; a patron.

Mujeebah: مجيبه

(Mujibah) One who answers; one who accepts or grants something.

Mukarrmah: مكرمه

Honorable; graceful; excellent.

Mu'minah: مومنه

The believer; one who embraced Islam by heart.

Mumtaaz: ممتاز

Outstanding; distinguished; exalted; illustrious; eminent; chosen.

Munawwarah: منوره

Brilliant; illuminated; enlightened; splendid.

Muneebah: منيبه

One who turns to Allah; a master; a patron; an agent; a client.

Muneerah: منيره

Brilliant; splendid; illuminating; enlightened; splendid.

Mu'nisah: مؤنسه

A companion; a comrade; an associate.

Munjiyah: منجيه

A woman who saves someone.

Munyah: مُنيه

Wish; desire.

Muqaddasah: مقدسه

Holy; sacred

Murdiyyah: مرضيه

(Murzyah) Chosen; liked; approved; desirable; pleasing; laudable; favorite.

Muslimah: مسلمة

Submitting to Allah, a Muslim woman.

Musta'eenah: مستعينة

Praying for help; soliciting aid.

Muzainah: مُزَينة

A small drizzling cloud, Name of a Sahabiyyah (RA); Name of an Arab tribe.

Muznah: مُزنة

A drizzling cloud, Name of a Sahabiyy-
ah(RA).

Naabigh: نابغ

Distinguished; talented; man of genius, brilliant person.

Naadir: نادر

Rare; wonderful; uncommon; unique; precious; unusual; curious.

Naadir: ناضر

(Naazir): Fresh.

Naafi': نافع

One who benefits others.

Naaib: نائب

A vice; a deputy; delegate; viceregent; attorney; assistant.

Naajid: ناجد

One who helps; brave.

Naaji: ناجى

Saver.

Naaqid: ناقد

A critic; a reviewer; a fault-finder.

Naasih: ناصح

An advisor; a sincere friend; a monitor; a counselor; a faithful minister; giving sound advice.

Naashit: ناشط

Lively; brisk; active; energetic.

Naasir: ناصر

A helper; a friend ; Name of a well known emperor; Name of a Sahabi (RA).

Naatiq: ناطق

Speaker; a rational being;Decisive; rational; definite.

Naayaab: ناياب

(Persian) Rare; precious.

Naazhim: ناظم

(Naazim): Administrator; manager.

Naazhir: ناظر

(Naazir): Spectator; seer.

Nabeel: نبيل

Handsome; intelligint; dexterous; one who is skilled in archery.

Nadeem: نديم

Friend; colleague.

Nadheer: نذير

(Nazeer): A warner; a courtier; title of the Holy Prophet ﷺ.

Na'eem: نعيم

Ease; comfort; grace; blessing.

Nafaasat: نفاست

Precariousness.

Nafees: نفيس

Precious; choice; Noble.

Najeeb: نجيب

Excellent; noble; generous; praise-worthy; of noble family, honorable.

Najeed: نجید

> Brave ; lion; a person who does such deeds which other could not do.

Najm: نجم

> Star; a planet; Suitable name: Muhammad Najm; Najmuddin; Najmulhasan.

Naqeeb: نقیب

> A leader; guide; director; chairman; dean; principle; president; corporation, lawyer.

Naqi: نقی

> Pure; clean; clear; limpid.

Naseem: نسیم

> Air; breeze.

Naseer: نصیر

> A helper; a friend; name of a Sahabi(RA).

Nashaat: نشاط

> Gladness; joy; pleasure; cheerfulness; sprightliness.

Nasr: نصر

> Help.

Naweed: نوید

> (Persian) Good news; glad tidings.

Nawfal: نوفل

> Name of a Sahabi(RA).

Nazaakat : نزاکت

> Delicacy; neatness; elegance; politeness; softness.

Nazheef: نظیف

> (Nazeef): Clean; neat; chaste.

Nazheer: نظیر

(Nazeer) Example; instance; precedent.

Nihaal: نهال

(Persian) A young; planet; pleased; happy; prosperous.

Nithaar: نثار

(Nisaar): Scattering; throwing; strewing; dispersion; sacrifice; money which is thrown to the poor people on festive occasions.

Niyaaz: نياز

(Persian) Supplication; a thing dedicated; an offering; acquaintance; meeting.

Nizhaam: نظام

(Nizaam): System; rule.

Nooh: نوح

Name of a well-known prophet of Allah Almighty.

Noor: نور

Light; splendor.

Noshaad: نوشاد

(Persian) Happy.

Nu'aimaan: نعيمان

Name of a Sahabi who participated in the battle of Badr.

Nu'maan: نعمان

Name of a Sahabi who participated in the battle of Badr.

Noor: نور

Light; splendor.

Noshaad: نوشاد

(Persian) Happy.

Female Names

Naadirah: ناضره

(Nazirah): One with healthy and happy looks;
a bright face reflecting luster and freshness.

Naadirah: نادره
Rare; choice; precious.

Naafi'ah: نافعه
Profitable; advantagious; useful; beneficial;
good.

Naa'ilah: نائله
Earner; winner.

Naajiya: ناجيه
One who saves oneself; One who gets salvation.

Naajidah: ناجده

Courageous; a lady who accomplishes difficult
tasks. one who appeals for help or takes liber-
ties.

Naasihah: ناصحه
An advisor; a sincere friend; a monitor; a
counselor; a faithful minister; giving sound
advice.

Naashitah: ناشطه
Lively; brisk; active; energetic.

Naasirah: ناصره

A helper; a friend.

Naayaab: ناياب

(Persian) Rare; precious.

Naazhimah: ناظمه

(Naazimah) Administrator; manager.

Naazhirah: ناظره

(Naazirah) Fresh; spectator; seer.

Nabeelah: نبيله

Beautiful; intelligent; dexterous.

Nadeemah: نديمه

A companion; friend.

Na'eemah: نعيمه

Ease; comfort; grace; blessing.

Nafeesah: نفيسه

Precious; choice; exquisite; delicate; refined; pure.

Nageenah: نگينه

(Persian) Precious stone.

Najeebah: نجيبه

Excellent; noble; generous; praiseworthy.

Najeedah: نجيده

Brave; a lady who accomplishes difficult tasks.

Najm: نجم
Star; a planet.

Najmah: نجمه
A star; planet.

Nakhat: نکهت
Perfume; scent.

Nashaat: نشاط
Gladness; joy; pleasure; cheerfulness; sprightliness.

Naqeebah: نقیبه
A leader; guide; director; dean; principle.

Nargis: نرگس
(Persian) Narcissus; a flower.

Naseemah: نسیمه
Air; breeze.

Naseerah: نصیره
A helper; a friend.

Naashirah: ناشرة
A helper; a friend.

Nasreen: نسرین
(Persian) A weld rose; the jonquil.

Naweed: نوید

Good news; glad tidings; invitation to a wedding (to kinsfolk and brethren).

Nawailah: نویله

a gift.

Nayyirah: نیّره

Luminary; shedding light; a bright star.

Nazaakat : نزاکت

(Persian) Delicacy; neatness; elegance; politeness; softness.

Nadheerah: نذیره

Anything offered as a token of respect; anything given as sacrifice; a child who has been dedicated by his parents to serve Allah.

Nazheerah: نظیره

(Nazeerah): Example; instance; precedent.

Nazheefah: نظیفه

(Nazeefah) Pure; neat; clean; legal.

Neelofar: نیلوفر

(Persian) The lotus; water-lily.

Ni'mat: نعمت

Blessing; boon; grace; comforts of life.

Noshaabah: نوشابه

(Persian) Water of life; elixir.

Nudrat: ندرت

uniqueness; singularity; rareness.

Nusrat: نصرت

Help; victory.

Nuzhat: نزهت

Freshness; pleasure; delight; cheerfulness; purity.

Qaadir: قادر

Powerful; mighty; an attribute applied to Allah Almighty. Name: AbdulQaadir.

Qaasim: قاسم

One who distributes; name of the beloved son of Rasoolullah Sallallaahu-alayhi-wasallam; also his attribute.

Qaani': قانع

Satisfied; contented.

Qaanit: قانت

Obedient to God; devout; silent.

Qaaim: قائم

Standing person, steadfast.

Qaazi: قاضى

(Qaaḍi) Judge; Justice.

Qaabeel: قابيل

Famous son of Adam (Adam) Alayhesalam.

Qadeer : قدير

Powerful; mighty ; an attribute exclusively applied to Allah, Name AbdulQuadeer.

Qais: قيس

Name of a Sahabi who took part in the battle of Badr; was the chief security guard of the Holy Prophet peace be upon him.

Qamar: قمر

Moon.

Qareeb: قريب

Near.

Qaseem: قسيم

Category.

Qaṣid: قاصد

A messenger; courier; envoy.

Qataadah: قتاده

Name of a Sahabi who took part in the battle of Badr.

Qawiyy: قوى

Strong; powerful; firm; an attribute of Allah Almighty. Name: abdul Quaawiyy.

Qudaamah: قُدامة

Name of a Sahabi who took part in the battle of Badr.

Qurbaan: قربان

Sacrifice; an offering.

Qutaibah: قتيبه

Name of a great Mujahid (warrior) in the way of Allah and name of a Ṣahabi.

Quṭbah: قطبه

Name of a Sahabi who took part in the battle of Badr.

Qutb: قطب

The iron spindle or axis on which a millstone turns; the polar star; a title or degree of rank among religious mendicants; a pivot; a lord; a chief.

Female Names

Parween: پروین
(Persian) Cluster of small stars; brilliant group of persons or things.

Qaani'ah: قانعه
Satisfied; contented.

Qaailah: قائله
Name of a Sahabiyyah(RA).

Qareebah: قریبه
Near.

Qailah: قیله
Name of a Sahabiyyah (RA).

Qamar: قمر
The moon .

Quddoosiyyah: قدّوسیه
A girl who is free from any physical or moral defects; a blessed girl. a pious girl; celestial.

Qudsiyah: قُدسیه
Holy; celestial.

Qurratul'ain: قرة العین
Freshening the eye; cool of eye.

Raabi'ah: رابعه
A bounding in green foliage. Name of a Sahabi who took part in the battle of Badr.

Raabit: رابط
One who connects between two things.

Raadi: راضى
(Raazi) Agreed; contended; willing; satisfied; pleased.

Raafi': رافع
Name of a Sahabi who took part in the battle of Badr.

Raaghib: راغب
Willing; wishing; desirous; inclined towards.

Raahat: راحت
Comfort; rest; ease; tranquillity; relief; pleasure.

Raashid: راشد
Pious; follower of the right path.

Rabah: رباح
Name of a Sahabi(RA).

Rabbaani: ربانى
Divine; Godly.

Rabee': ربيع
Spring.

Radi: رضى
(Razi): Agreed; contented; pleased.

Ra'ees: رئيس

Rich; wealthy.

Rafeeq: رفيق

Friend; colleague.

Rafee': رفيع

High, exalted, of nobility and dignity.

Raheem: رحيم

Allah's attribute: Most Merciful, Most kind.
Names: Abdur-Raheem, Muhammad Raheem,
Fazlur Raheem.

Rahmaan: رحمن

Allah's attribute meaning :Most Merciful,
Most kind ,suitable combination of names are:
Abdul Rahmaan, AzeezurRahmaan, Ahmadur
Rahmaan, Khaleelurrahmaan.

Rahmat: رحمت

(Rahmah) mercy.

Raihan: ريحان

A sweet smelling plant; any flower besides
rose; comfort.

Rajaa': رجاء

Name of a Sahabi(RA).

Rakhshaan: رخشان

(Persian) Dazzling; resplendent.

Rauoof: رؤف

An attribute applied to Allah, meaning :Most
Merciful, Most kind ; the prophet Muhammad
peace be upon him was also referred to as
Raoof by the Holy Quraan. Name: Abdur-
Raoof.

Raqueeb: رقيب
    Guardian.

Raseem: رسيم
    Name of a Sahabi (RA).

Rashad: رشاد
    Guidance; a righteous life.

Rashdan: رشدان
    Name of a Sahabi(RA).

Rasheed: رشيد
    Follower of the right path; intelligent.

Raudah: روضه
    (Rauzah): Paradise.

Rauh: روح
    Name of a Sahabi(RA).

Raumaan: رومان
    Name of a Sahabi(RA).

Rawaha: رواحه
    Name of a person.

Razeen: رزين
    Gentle, Noble, Name of a Sahabi.

Razzaaq: رزاق
    Allah's Attribute meaning the provider, the sustainer . Name: AbdurRazzaaq.

Rib'i: ربعى
    Name of a Sahabi who took part in the battle of Badr.

Ridaa': رضاء
    (Rizaa'): Pleasure; contentment; approval; leave; permission; assent.

Ridwaan: رضوان

(Rizwaan); Pleasure; contentment; approval;
leave; permission; assent; name of an overseer
of Jannat, paradise.

Rif'ah: رفاعه

(Rifa'at): Highness; elevation;dignity. Name of
a Sahabi who took part in the battle of Badr.

Riyaad: رياض

(Riyaaz) (pl.. of Rauzah) Garden; meadow.

Riyasat: رياست

Government; dominion; sway; rule; nobility;
high mindedness.

Ronaq: رونق

Luster; brightness; elegance; beauty; symme-
try; color; splendor; freshness; flashing state or
condition.

Roshan: روشن

(Persian) Bright; luster; shining.

Rukanah: ركانه

Name of a Sahabi(RA).

Rukhailah: رخيله

Name of a Sahabi who took part in the battle
of Badr.

Rushd: رشد

To be on the right way; not to go astray; to be
a true believer; to be or become mature or sensible.

Ruwaifi': رويفع

Name of a distinguished Sahabi (RA).

Female Names

Raabi'a: رابعه

Residing peacefully; Name of a Sahabiyy-ah(RA); Name of a saint who is known as Rabiah Basriyyah.

Raabitah: رابطه

Connection.

Raafi'ah: رافعه

High; exalted; wealthy.

Raahat: راحت

Comfort; rest; ease; tranquillity; relief; pleasure.

Raahilah: راحله

A travelling woman.

Raa'iqhah: رائقه

Charming.

Raani: رانى

(Urdu) A queen.

Raashidah: راشده

Pious; follower of the right path.

Raaziyah: راضيه

(Raadiyah) Agreed; willing; satisfied; pleased.

Rabee'ah: ربيعه

A bounding in green foliage. Name of a Sahabi who took part in the battle of Badr.

Radiyyah: رضيه

(Raziyyah): Pleased; delighted; contented.

Ra'eesah: رئيسه
> Leader; chief; princess; a noble lady; a wealthy lady; Rich.

Rafee'ah: رفيعه
> High; exalted sublime; elevated.

Rafeeqah: رفيقه
> Friend; associate; companion; a soft and kind-hearted lady.

Raheemah: رحيمه
> Kind; affectionate.

Raihaana: ريحانه
> A sweet-smelling flower; name of a Sahabi(RA).

Raitah: ريطه
> Name of many Sahabiyyat (RA).

Rakheelah: رخيله
> Name of a Sahabi(RA).

Rakhshaan: رخشان
> (Persian) Dazzling; resplendent.

Rakhshindah: رخشنده
> (Persian) Bright; resplendent.

Rameesah: رميسه
> Name of a Sahabiyyah (RA).

Rameethah: رميثه
> Name of a Sahabiyyah (RA).

Ramlah: رمله
> Name of an Ummulmoomineen Hazrat Umm Habibah(RA), the wife of the prophet peace be upon him.

Ra'naa: رعنا
> Moving gracefully; lovely; beautiful; graceful; delicate; tender.

Raodah:روضه
> (Raozah) Park.

Raqeebah: رقيبه
> Guardian.

Rashaad:رشاد
> Guidance; a righteous life.

Rasheedah: رشيده
> Follower of the right path , intellegent.

Raunaq: رونق
> (Persian): Luster; brightness; elegance; beauty; symmetry; color; splendor; freshness; flashing state or condition.

Raushan: روشن
> (Persian) Bright; luster; shining.

Rawahah: رواحه
> Name of a person.

Razeenah: رزينه
> Name of a Sahabiyah(RA).

Ribqah: ربقه
> The wife of Hzrat Ishaaq (Ishacc) peace be upon him, a prophet of Allah Almighty.

Rifa'at: رفعت
> Highness; elevation;diginity.

Ridwaanah: رضوانه
> (Rizwaanah); Pleasure; delighted; content.

Rida: رضا

> (Rizaa): Pleasure; contentment; approval; Pleasure; contentment; approval; leave; permission; assent.

Romaan: رومان

> Name of a Sahabi(RA).

Rufaidah: رُفيده

> Name of a Sahabiyyah who gave treatment to the injured in a hut of the mosque.

Rukhailah: رُخيله

> Name of a Sahabi who took part in the battle of Badr.

Rukhsaanah: رخسانه

> (persian) Name of a girl.

Rumaithah: رُميثه

> Name of a Sahabiyah(RA).

Rummanah: رُمّانه

> A pomegranate.

Ruqayyah: رقيه

> Name of the daughter of the Holy Prophet peace be upon him.

 ث س ش ص

Sa'aadat: سعادت
(Saadah) Fortune; blessings; victory.

Sa'd: سعد
Name of a Sahabi who took part in the battle of Badr.

Sa'daan: سعدان
Happier, luckier.

Saa'id: ساعد
Name of a Sahabi (RA).

Saabiq: سابق
The first in a race, Name of a Sahabi (RA) who was the servant of the Holy Prophet peace be upon him.

Saabit: ثابت
(Thaabit): Name of a Sahabi(RA).

Saabir: صابر
One who patienly and stoically edures all hardships and diffichlties; title of Ayyoob
(عليه السلام).

Saadiq: صادق
True; sincere; faithful; veracious; a man of his word.

Saahib: صاحب
Friend; colleague.

Saaib: سائب

Name of a Sahabi who took part in the battle of Badr.

Saaim: صائم

Name of a Sahabi who took part in the battle of Badr.

Saa'irah: سائره

Name of a Sahabi (RA).

Saajid: ساجد

One who makes sajdah (prostration).

Saalif: سالف

Name of a Sahabi (RA).

Saalih: صالح

Virtuous; chaste; righteous; name of a well-known prophet fo Allah.

Saalik: سالك

Proceeding.

Saalim: سالم

Name of a Sahabi (RA); a famous jurist.

Saamit: صامت

Name of a Sahabi (RA).

Sabaahat: صباحت

Beauty.

Sablah: صباح

Morning; dawn; day-break.

Sabeeh: صبيح

Name of a Sahabi (RA); Beautiful; handsome.

Saboor: صبور

Patient ; fore bearing; one who overlooks the fault of others.

Saburah: سبرة

> Name of a Sahabi who took part in the battle of Badr.

Sadaaqat: صداقت

> Truth.

Sadeed: سديد

> Right; correct; hitting the target; apposite.

Sadeem: سديم

> Mist; haze; nebula.

Sadeeq: صديق

> Friend; colleague.

Sadr: صدر

> chest; breast; bosom; the hiehest part; the hiehest peson; chief; suitable combination: Sadruddeen.

Sa'eed: سعيد

> Fortunate; lucky; :Name of a Sahabi who took part in the battle of Badr.

Safdar: صفدر

> A warrior; brave.

Safeena: سفينه

> A boat (Safeenah) Name of a slave of the Holy Prophet peace be upon him.

Safeer: سفير

> Counsel; messenger; deputy.

Safyy: صفى

> Chosen, Name of a Sahabi (RA).

Safwaan: صفوان

> A rock, Name of a Sahabi (RA).

Sagheer: صغير
  Little; short.

Sahaab: سحاب
  Cloud; mist.

Shahrukh: شاه رخ
  (Persian) Name of a man.

Sahl: سهل
  Name of a Sahabi who took part in the battle of Badr.

Sahm: سهم
  Name of a Sahabi (RA).

Sahar: سحر
  Name of a Sahabi(RA).

Saif: سيف
  Sword.

Saifiyy: سيفى
  Name of a Sahabi who took part in the battle of Badr.

Saihaan: سيحان
  Flowing, Name of a Sahabi (RA).

Sajjaad: سجاد
  Prostrating in the prayer; one who makes Sajdah in the Salah.

Sakhawat: سخاوت
  Generosity; liberality; munificence; charity.

Sakhr: صخر
  Rock; Name of a Sahabi who took part in the battle of Badr.

Sakhrah: صخرة

Name of a Sahabi (RA).

Salaah: صلاح

Goodness of state or condition; prosperity; piety.

Salaamat: سلامت

Safety.

Salaam: سلام

(Salaam)Salutation; peace; safety; compliment; good-bye; Name of a Sahabi (RA).

Salamah: سلمه

Name of a Sahabi who took part in the battle of Badr.

Sulaik:سليك

Name of a Sahabi (RA).

Saleem: سليم

Pacific; mild; affable; perfect; healthy.

Saleet: سَليط

Name of Sahabi who was the messenger of the prophet peace be upon him to the ruler of Ya-mamah.

Sallaam: سلّام

Very safe; well; sound.

Salmaan: سلمان

Name of a distinguished Sahabi (RA).

Saman: ثمن

(Thaman) Price; fare; cost.

Samar: ثمر

(Thamar) Fruit.

Sameen: ثمين

   (Thameen) Precious; costly; dear.

Sameer: سمير

   Companion in nightly entertainment, conversation Partner; entertainer. Sameer: Name of a Sahabi (RA).

Samee': سميع

   The all-Hearing; He who hears every thing. Names;Abdus Samee'.

Samsaam: صمصام

   Sword; Name: Samsaamuddin.

Samurah: سمره

   Name of a distinguished Sahabi (RA).

Sinaan: سنان

   Blade of a spear. Name of a Sahabi (RA).

Sanaubar: صنوبر

   A cone-bearing tree; pine-tree.

Sa'ood: سعود

   Lucky, fortunate.

Saarah: ساره

   Name of the wife of Hazrat Ibrahim (peace be upon him) , the prophet of Allah Almighty.

Sarmad: سرمد

   Eternal; perpetual; everlasting.

Sarwaat: ثروت

   (Tharwat) Wealth; power; influence; affluence.

Sarwar: سرور

   A chief; a leader; lord; master.

Sattaar: ستّار

An attribute of Allah, meaning : one who conceals faults ....by the veil of His Mercy.
Name ; AbdusSattaar.

Saulat: صولت

(Urdu) awfulness.

Sawaa': سواء

Name of a Sahabi (RA).

Sawaad: سودا

Name of a Sahabi who took part in the battle
of Badr.

Sawwaaf: صوّاف

Wool merchant.

Sayyaar: سيّار

Name of a distinguished Sahabi (RA).

Sayyid: سيد

Lord; master; chief; leader.

Seemaa: سيما

Sign; Face; forehead; similitude; countenance.

Shaafee: شافي

Heeler; restorer of health; one of the attuibutes
of Almighty Allah.

Shaabah: شابه

Name of a Sahabi (RA).

Shaad: شاد

(Persian) Happy; pleased.

Shaadaan: شادان

Happy; pleased.

Shaafi': شافع

One who intercedes; a mediator; Name of a

Sahabi (RA).

Shaafi: شافى

Healer; Restorer of health; one of the attributes of Allah.

Shaah: شاه

King; monarch; emperor.

Shaaheen: شاهين

A royal white falcon.

Shaahid: شاهد

One who bears witness; a deponent.

Shaakir: شاكر

Grateful; thankful; content; praising.

Shaan: شان

Condition; business; affair; state; dignity; quality; nature; disposition; luster; eminence; glory; grandeur.

Shaariq: شارق

Radiant; shining.

Shabaab: شباب

Youth; prime of life; Name of a Sahabi.

Shabb: شاب

Young.

Shabeeh: شبيه

Similar; likeness image; resemblance.

Shabbeer: شبّير

Beautiful; virtuous; dignified; title of Imaam Husain (RA).

shafa'at: شفاعت

Intercession; recommendation; entreaty.

Shafee': شفيع

Intercessor.

Shafeeq: شفيق

Affectionate; compassionate; a kind hearted friend.

Shafqat: شفقت

Kindness; affection; favour; mercy; clemency ; compassion; condolence.

Shaguftah: شگفته

Expanded; blown; blooming; flourishing.

Shihaab: شهاب

A star.

Shaheed: شهيد

Present; witness; one who gives evidence based on truth; a martyr.

Shaheer: شهير

Eminent; famous; popular.

Shaibah: شيبه

Name of a Sahabi (RA).

Shaibaan: شيبان

Name of a Sahabi (RA).

Shajee': شجيع

Brave; bold; fearless.

Shakeel: شکيل

Beautiful.

Shakoor: شکور

Most grateful; one who gives due appreciation; one who can appreciate the worth of any deed; an attribute of Allah.

Shameem: شميم

Fragrant; scent; a sweet-smelling breeze.

Shammaas: شمَّاس

Name of a Sahabi who took part in the battle of Badr.

Shams: شمس

Sun.

Shamshaad: شمشاد

(Persian) The box tree; a tall and upright tree; the graceful figure of a beloved.

Sh`amsulhaq: شمس الحق

The sun of truth; Name of a great scholar in Pakistan.

Shaqeeq: شقيق

Real, Name of a Sahabi (RA); Part; half; piece; brother.

Sharaf: شرف

Honor; honor and esteem due to some meritorious achievement.

Sharaafat: شرافت

Nobility; illustrious; to be distinguished.

Shareef: شريف

Noble , eminent ; legitimate; chief of a tribe ; one with honorable family back grownd; urbane.

Shareek: شريك

Partner; Name of a Sahabi (RA).

Shaukat: شوكت

Dignity; magnificence; grandeur; power.

Shehryaar: شهريار

(Persian) Name of a man.

Shibli: شبلى

Name of a great saint.

Shifaa': شفاء

Cure; healing; recovery; convalescence.

Shu'aib: شعيب

Name of a prophet of Allah Almighty.

Shu'aa': شعاع

The rays of the sun; sunshine; light; luster; splendor.

Shujaa': شجاع

Name of a Sahabi who took part in the battle of Badr; and who was sent to Damascus as a messenger by the Holy Prophet peace be upon him.

Shujaa'at: شجاعت

Bravery; valor; fearlessness.

Shuqraan: شقران

Name of a Sahabi who took part in the battle of Badr;and he was the freed slave of the Holy Prophet peace be upon him.

Sharaaheel: شراحيل

Name of a Sahabi (RA).

Shurahbeel: شرحبيل

Name of a distinguished Sahabi (RA) who conquered Jorden.

Shuraih: شُريح

Name of a Sahabi (RA).

Siddeeq: صدّيق

Title of the caliph Abu Bakr (RA); truthful; righteous.

Sikandar: سكندر
Alexander.

Silaah: سلاح
Arms; armour; weapos; suitable combination:
Silaahuddeen.

Simaak: سماك
Name of a Sahabi (RA).

Siraaj: سراج
A lamp; the sun; a candle.

Siwaar: سوار
Name of a Sahabi (RA).

Subaih: صبيح
Name of a Sahabi who took part in the battle
of Badr.

Subbooh: سبوح
Extremely pure; Allah's attribute. Name: Ab-
dus-Subbooh.

Sufyaan: سفيان
Name of a great Sahabi(RA).

Suhaib: صهيب
Name of a Sahabi who took part in the battle
of Badr.

Suhail: سهيل
Name of a Sahabi (RA); The star Canopus; the
star

Sulaimaan: سليمان
Name of the famous prophet of Allah Almighty; his English equivalent is Solomon.

Sulait: سُلَيْط

    Name of a Sahabi(RA).

Suraquah: سُراقه

    Name of a Sahabi (RA).

Surraaq: سُرّاق

    Name of a distinguished Sahabi (RA)

Suwaibit: سويبط

    Name of a Sahabi(RA).

Suwaid: سويد

    Name of a Sahabi(RA).

Female Names

Saabiqah: سابقه

Precedent; one who comes first in a race;
Name of a Sahabi (RA) who was the servant of
the Holy Prophet peace be upon him;

Sa'aadat: سعادت

(Sa'aadah) Fortune; blessings; victory.

Saabirah: صابره

Patient; tolorant.

Saadiqhah: صادقه

True; sincere; faithful; veracious; a woman of
his word.

Saahibah: صاحبه

Friend; colleague.

Saahirah: ساهرة

Earth; moon; a spring which flows constantly.

Saa'imah: صائمه

Fasting woman.

Saa'irah: سائره

Name of a Sahabiyyah (RA).

Saajidah: ساجده

Prostrating in prayer (salah); one who makes
sajdah.

Saalifah: سالفه

Previous, last.

Saalihah: صالحه

Pious, righteous.

Saalikah: سالكه

Following; proceeding.

Saarah: سارة

(Saarah) The wife of Hazrat Ibrahim عليه السلام the prophet of Allah.

Saariyah: سارية

Name of a Sahabiyyah (RA).

Saarrah: سارّة

A lady whose carming manner causes joy and happiness.

Sabaa: صبا

A gentle breeze; an easterly breeze; a morning breeze; zephyr.

Sabaahat: صباحت

Beauty; gracefulness; comeliness.

Sabeehah: صبيحه

Beautiful; handsome.

Saburah: سَبُرة

Name of a Sahabi who took part in the battle of Badr.

Sadaaqat: صداقت

Truth.

Sadaf: صدف

Shell; a mother of pearl.

Sa'diyah: سعديه

Blessed; Title of the lady who had breast fed Rasoolullah sallallahu alaihe wasallam- Full name: Halimah Sa'diah.

Sa'eedah: سعيده

Fortunate; lucky.

Safeenah: سفينه

A boat, Name of a slave of the prophet peace be upon him.

Safeerah: سفيره

Counsel; messenger; deputy.

Safooraa': صفوره

Name of the wife of Hazrat Moosa (peace be upon him).

Safiyyah: صفيه

Chosen, Name of an Ummulmoomineen, the wife of the Holy Prophet peace be upon him.

Sagheerah : صغيره

Little; short.

Sahlah: سهله

Name of a Sahabiyyah(RA); Easy; convenient.

Sahar: سحر

Name of a Sahabi(RA).

Sakeenah: سكينه
Content; accord; pleasure.

Sakhaawat: سخاوت
Generosity; liberality; munificence; charity.

Salaamah: سلامه
Salvation; peace; free from blemish; ease;
name of a Sahaabi (RA)

Saleemah: سليمه
Perfect; healthy.

Salmaa: سلمى
Safe; free; sound; healthy.

Saman: ثمن
(Thaman) Price; fare; cost;(Saman).

Samar: ثمر
(Thamar) Fruit.

Sameenah: سمينه
A healthy girl; fertile land without rock and
stone.

Sameenah: ثمينه
(Thameenah) Expensive; precious; costly;
dear.

Sameerah: سميره
Companion in nightly entertainment, conversation partner; entertainer.

Samee'ah: سميعه

Hearing; she who hears .

Sanaa': ثناء

(Thana):Praise of God.

Sanjeedah: سنجیده

(Persian) Calm; grave; matured, weighty; considerate; composed; serious: approved.

Sanaubar: صنوبر

A cone-bearing tree; pine-tree.

Saarah: سارا

Name of the wife of Hazrat Ibrahim (peace be upon him) , a prophet of Allah Almighty.

Sarwaat: ثروت

(Tharwat) Wealth; power; influence; affluence.

Sarwar: سرور

(Persian) A chief; a leader; lord; master.

Sarwari: سروری

(Persian) Chiefship; sovereignty; rule; sway.

Saudah: سوده

Name of one of the honourable wives of the Holy prophet ﴾ﷺ﴿ .

Sayyidah: سیده

Name of the wife of Hazrat Ismaa'il (Ishmeel) peace be upon him, a prophet of Allah Almighty.

Seema: سیما

Sign; Face; forehead; similitude; countenance; aspect.

Seemeen: سیمین

(Persian) of silver; silvery; white.

Shaad: شاد

(Persian) Happy; pleased.

Shaadan: شادان

(Persian) Happy; pleased.

Shaafi'ah: شافعه

One who deprecates; one who intercedes; advocate; patron; a mediator.

Shaaheen: شاهین

A royal white falcon.

Shaahidah: شاهده

One who bears witness; a deponent.

Shaaheenah: شاهینه

A royal white falcon.

Shaaistah: شائسته

(Persian) Polite.

Shaakirah: شاکره

Grateful (for); thankful; content; praising; one who gives due appreciation.

Shaariqah: شارقة

Radiant; shining.

Shabeehah: شبيهة

Similar; picture; portrait; likeness image; resemblance.

Shabnam: شبنم

(Persian) Dew; a kind of fine linen.

Shafee'ah: شفيعة

Advocate; patron; intercessor.

Shafeeqah: شفيقة

Affectionate; compassionate; a kind hearted friend.

Shafqat: شفقت

Kindness; affection; favour; mercy; clemency; compassion; condolence.

Shaguftah: شگفته

(Persian) Expanded; blown; blooming; flourishing.

Shahlaa': شهلا

Having grey eyes with a shade of red; a species of Nacissus flower.

Shaheerah: شهيرة

Eminent; famous, popular.

Shahnaaz: شهناز

(Persian) Name of a flower.

Shajarah: شجرة
  Tree; name of an Egyptian woman ruler.

Shajaratuddurr: شجرة الدر
  Name of an Egyptian woman ruler.

Sahjee'ah: شجيعه
  Brave; bold; courageous.

Shakeelah: شكيله
  Pretty girl.

Sham': شمع
  A lamp; a candle.

Shamaailah: شمائله
  Good qualities; virtues; excellencies; talents;·
  dispositions; customs; northerly winds or regions.

Shameelah: شميله
  Good quality; virtue; excellence; talent; disposition; custom; northerly winds or regions.

Shamaamah: شمامه
  The fragrance of scent; perfume.

Shameemah: شميمه
  Fragrant; scent; a sweet-smelling breeze; lofty.
  Name: Shameemah.

Shmoodah: شموده
  Diamond.

Shaqeeqah: شقيقه

Real sister.

Shareefah: شريفه

Noble , eminent ; legitimate; chief of a tribe ; one with honorable family back ground; urbane.

Sharfaa': شرفآء

A most noble and honourable lady; name of a Sahabiyyah.

Shareekah: شريکه

Participant, partner.

Shareefah: شريفه

Noble; holy; modest; humble.

Sheereen: شيرين

(Persian) Sweet; Name of a queen of Iran.

Shu'aa': شعاع

The rays of the sun; sunshine; light; luster; splendor.

Siddeeqah: صديقه

truthful; righteous.

Sidrah: سدره

Name of a tree. Name of a Sahabiyyah (RA).

Sitaarah: ستارة

(Persian) Star; a planet.

Sughraa: صغرى

Small; slender; tender.

Suhailah: سُهيله

The star Canopies; the star.

Sukainah: سُكينه

Diminutive of Sakeenah ; meaning is same as Sakeenah.

Sultaanah: سلطانه

Queen; empress.

Sumairaa': سميره

Of a brownish colour; Name of a Sahabiyyah (RA).

Sumayyah: سُميّه

Name of a Sahabiyyah(RA).

Surayyaa: ثريا

Cluster of seven brilliant stars in Taurus, commonly known as the seven sisters; a wealthy lady; luster; chandelier.

Suwaibah: ثويبه

(Thuwaibah) Name of the woman who breast-fed the Holy Prophet (Peace be upon him) in his infaney.

Taabish: تابش

(Persian) Heat; splendor; brilliance.

Tasadduq: تصدّق

To give Sadaqah or alms; to sacrifice; to strew generously.

Taaha: طه

Name of a Surah in the Holy Quraan.

Taahir: طاهر

Clean; Name of a son of the Holy Prophet peace be upon him.

Taaj: تاج

Crown.

Taali': طالع

One who ascends, the star of luck.

Taalib: طالب

A seeker; an inquirer; a lover.

Taariq: طارق

The morning star; a night- traveller; name of a great Muslim general who conqrered Spain. jabal- al- Taariq which has been changed to Gibraltar is named after him, also the name of a Sahabi(RA).

Taaseen: طاسين

A name of the Holy prophet Muhammad Peace be upon him.

Taabaan: تابان

(Persian) Resplendent; splendid; glittering; refulgent; burning.

Tabassum: تبسم

Smiling; a smile.

Tahawwur: تهوّر

Temerity; rashness; intrepidity.

Tahoor: طهور

Purifying.

Tahseen: تحسين

Approbation; applause; acclamation; cheers.

Tajammul: تجمل

Dignity; magnificence.

Tal'at: طلعت

Appearance; countenance; face; aspect.

Talhah: طلحه

Name of a distinguished Sahabi (RA), one of the ten who were declared by the Holy Prophet (peace be upon him) as the people of Jannah.

Tamannaa: تمنّا

Desire; wish; want.

Tameem: تميم

Name of a Sahabi who participated in the battle of Badr.

Tameez: تميز

(Urdu) Discernment; judgment; discretion; distinction; observance of rules of etiquette.

Tamkeen: تمكين
Majesty; dignity; authority; power.

Tanweer: تنوير
Illuminating;enlightening; illumination.

Taqiyy: تقى
Pious; devout.

Tarannum: ترنم
A kind of song; modulation.

Tasawwur: تصور
Imagination;contemplation;meditation; reflection; fancy;idea; conception; preconception; apprehension.

Tasneem: تسنيم
A fountain of Paradise.

Tawfeeq: توفيق
Adaptation; accommodation; reconciliation; mediation; arbitration; success (granted by Allah)happy out come; good; fortune; prosperity; succeeding.

Tawoos: طاؤس
A peacocks the name of a famous tabi'i.

Tawqeer: توقير
Honor; respect; reverence; veneration.

Tawwaab: تواب
Acceptor of repentance; Allah's attribute.

Tayyib: طيب

> Good; Name of the son the prophet peace be upon him.

Thaabit: ثابت

> (Saabit): Name of a Sahabi who participated in the battle of Badr .

Thaaqib: ثاقب

> (Saaqib): Shining brightly; glistening; splendid. Name: Thaaqib Husain and Thaaqib Ahmed.

Tha'labah: ثعلبه

> (Sa'alabah); Name of a Sahabi who participated in the battle of Badr.

Thaman: ثمن

> (Saman) Price; fare; cost.

Thamar: ثمر

> (Samar) Fruit.

Thameen: ثمين

> (Sameen) Precious; costly; dear.

Thaqaf: ثقف

> (Saqaf): Name of a Sahabi who participated in the battle of Badr.

Tharwaat: ثروت

> (Sarwat) Wealth; power; influence; affluence.

Thaubaan: ثوبان

>   (Saubaan): Name of a distinguished Sahabi
>   (RA).

Thumamah: ثمامة

>   (Sumamah): Name of a distinguished Sahabi
>   (RA)

ihaami: تهامى

>   One who lives in Tihamah, a place in Arab, a
>   title of the Holy Prophet (peace be upon him).

Tooba: طوبى

>   Glad tiding; good news.

Tauqeer: توقير

>   Honor; respect: reverence; veneration.

Tauseef: توصيف

>   Description;commendation;describing; qualif-
>   ying.

Tufail: طفيل

>   Name of a Sahabi who participated in the
>   battle of Badr.

Tulaib: طليب

>   Name of a Sahabi who participated in the
>   battle of Badr.

Female Names

Taahirah: طاهره

Clean.

Taa'ibah: تائبه

One who refrains from evil-doings; repentant.

Taaj: تاج

Crown.

Taali'ah: طالع

Rising; star.

Taalibah: طالبه

A seeker; an inquirer; a lover.

Taaraa: تارا

(Urdu) Star.

Taabaan: تابان

(Persian) Resplendent; splendid; glittering; refulgent; burning.

Tabssum: تبسم

Smiling; a smile.

Tahseenah: تحسينه

Approbation; applause; acclamation; cheers.

Tal'at: طلعت

Appearance; countenance; face; aspect.

Tamannaa: تمنا

Desire; wish; want.

Tanweer: تنوير

Illuminating; inlightening; illumination.

Tarannum: ترنم

A kind of song; modulation.

Tawoos: طاؤس

A peacock.

Taybah: طيبه

Pure;chaste; pious; clean.

Tayyibah: طيّبه

Good.

Thuwaibah: ثو يبه

Name of a Sahabiyyah (RA); name of the lady who had breast-fed the Holy Prophet, Muhammad peace be upon him.

Thaman: ثمن

(Saman) Price; fare; cost;(Saman).

Thamar: ثمر

(Samar) Fruit.

Thameenah: ثمينه

(Sameen) Expensive; precious; costly; dear.

Thanaa': ثنا

Praise; applause; eulogy.

Tharwat: ثروت

Wealth; power; influence; affluence.

Thubaitah: ثبيته

Name of a Sahabiyyah (RA).

Thurayya: ثريا

Cluster of seven brilliant stars in Taurus, commonly known as the seven sisters; a wealthy lady; luster; chandelier.

Tooba: طوبى

Glad tiding; good news.

'Ubadah: عباده

Name of a Sahabi who took part in the battle of Badr.

'Ubayy: أبى

Name of a Sahabi who took part in the battle of Badr.

'Ubaid: عبيد

Name of a Sahabi who took part in the battle of Badr.

'Ubaidullah: عبيدالله

Little slave or servant of Allah.

'Ukashah: عكاشه

Name of a Sahabi who took part in the battle of Badr.

Ulfat: الفت

Friendship; intimacy; love; attachment; affection; familiarity.

'Umair: عمير

Name of a Sahabi who took part in the battle of Badr.

'Umar: عمر

Name of an illustrious Sahabi who was the second caliph of Islam.

'Umaarah: عماره

Name of a Sahabi who took part in the battle of Badr.

Unais: أنيس

Name of a Sahabi who took part in the battle of Badr.

'Uqbah: عتبه

Name of a famous Sahabi (RA).

'Urooj: عروج

Ascension; rising; exaltation; height.

'Urwah: عروه

Name of a Sahabi(RA).

Usamah: اسامة

A lion, Name of a famous Sahabi(RA).

Usaid: أسيد

A little lion, Name of a Sahabi who took part in the battle of Badr.

'Usmaan: عثمان

Well-known Sahabi and third caliph of the Holy Prophet, peace be upon him.

'Utbah: عتبه

Name of a Sahabi who took part in the battle of Badr.

'Uthmaan: عثمان

Name of a Sahabi who took part in the battle of Badr.

'Uwaim: عُويم

Name of a Sahabi who took part in the battle of Badr.

Uwais: اويس

Name of a great saint and Taabi'ee (RA).

'Uzair: عُزير

Name of a prophet of Allah Taala.

Female Names

Ulfat: الفت

Friendship; intimacy; love; attachment; affection; familiarity.

Umaimah: أميمة

Name of a Sahabiyyah (RA).

Umamah: امامة

Name of a Sahabiyyah(RA).

'Umarah: عُمارة

Name of a Sahabi who took part in the battle of Badr.

Umayyah: أميّة

Name of a Sahabiyyah(RA).

Umm Ayman: ام ايمن

She was a wet nurse of the Holy Prophet peace be upon him.

Umm Haani': ام هانى'

Name of a Sahabiyya(RA) who was a cousin of the Holy Prophet Muhammad peace be upon him, her name was Fakhtah.

Umm Kulthoom: ام كلثوم

Name of a daughter of the Holy Prophet peace be upon him.

Umm Abaan: أم أبان

Name of a Sahabiyyah (RA)

Umm fakeeh: ام فكيه

    Name of a Sahabiyyah (RA).

Umm Habibah: ام حبيبه

    Name of an Ummulmoomineen, the wife of the Holy Prophet peace be upon him.

Umm Haraam: ام حرام

    Name of a Sahabiyyah (RA).

Umm Rabee'ah: ام ربيعه

    Name of a Sahabiyyah (RA).

Umm Raumaan: أم رومان

    Name of a Sahabiyyah (RA) who was the wife of Hazrat Abu-Bakr (RA), second caliph of Islam.

Umm Salamah: ام سلمه

    Name of an Ummulmoomineen, the wife of the Holy Prophet peace be upon him.

Umm Shareek: ام شريك

    Name of a Sahabiyyah (RA).

Umm Sulaim: ام سليم

    Name of a Sahabiyyah (RA).

Umm Warqah: ام ورقه

    Name of a Sahabiyyah (RA).

Umm Yousuf: ام يوسف

    Name of a Sahabiyyah (RA).

Umm Khalid: ام خالد

    Name of a Sahabiyyah (RA).

Ummul Fazal: ام الفضل

Name of a Sahabiyyah (RA).

Umm'Umarah: أم عمارة

Name of a Sahabiyyah (RA).

Unaisah: أنيسه

Name of a Sahabiyyah(RA).

'Urooj: عروج

Ascension; rising; exaltation; height.

'Uzhmaa: عظمى

(Uzmaa): Greater; more dignified; more exalted.

 و

Waabiṣah: وابصه
Name of a distinguished Sahabi (RA).

Waahid: واحد
One; without partner; unique; an attribute applied to Allah Almighty.

Waa'izh: واعظ
(Waa'iz): A preacher; an adviser; a teacher; a monitor.

Waajid: واجد
One whose wants are satisfied; wealthy; a lover or beloved.

Waali: والى
The Governor;He who directs; manages; conducts; governs; measures.

Waaqif: واقف
Acquainted; aware of; experienced; conversant with; knowing; learned; sensible.

Waarid: وارد
Coming; arriving; approaching; alighting; descending; happening; being present.

Waarith: وارث
(Waaris)An heir; a master; a lord; an owner; a successor; The Supreme inheritor.

Waasi': واسع
(Waas') Capacious; wide; ample; One who possesses abundant (of anything) Allah's attribute; Meaning: The All Controlling.

Waasif: واصف

Describing.

Waasil: واصل

Joined; connected; coupled; arrived.

Waathiq: وائق

(Waasiq): Strong, firm; binding; confident; secure; confiding; Name of a caliph of Islam.

Waddood: ودود

Friend; companion; beloved; Allah's attribute. Name: AbdulWadod.

Wahaab: وهب

Gift; name of a Sahaabi(RA).

Wahbaan: وهبان

Name of a Sahabi (RA).

Waheed: وحيد

Unique; singular; unparalleled; alone.

Wahhaaj: وهّاج

Shinning; illuminated.

Wajaahat: وجاهت

High position; dignity; comeliness; respect; respectability; appearance; aspect.

Wajeeh: وجيه

Of a good appearance; handsome; respectable.

Wakaalat: وكالت

Leadership; advocacy; practice at the bar; attorneyship; embassy; agency; commission; proxy.

Wakee': وكيع

Name of the teacher of Hazrat Imam Shaafi' (RA).

Wakeel: وكيل

> The Trustee; He who provides a means to solve all problems in the best way.

Waleed: وليد

> Name of a caliph of Islam.

Waliyy: ولى

> The Protecting friend.

Waqaar: وقار

> Dignity; grace.

warqah: ورقه

> Name of a Sahabi(RA).

Wasiyy: وَصِى

> An executor; administrator (of a will); preceptor.

Waseef: وصيف

> Servant; page.

Waseem: وسيم

> Of a fine countenance; handsome; comely.

Wazeer: وزير

> A minister of state.

Wilaayat: ولايت

> An inhabited country; dominion; a foreign country; abroad; realm; possession; being master of anything; sovereignty; control; government; jurisdiction; guardianship; friendship; union(specially with God); sanctity; prophecy; the office of a saint.

Wuhaib: وُهيب

> A gift.

Female Names

Waahidah: واحده

One; unique.

Waajidah: واجده

A woman, who finds something, a happy woman.

Waaliyah: والیه

The female Governor; she who directs; manages; conducts; governs; measures.

Waarithah: وارثة

(Waarisah) An heir; a master; a lord; an owner; a successor.

Waasifah: واصفه

Describing.

Waasilah: واصله

Joining; connecting.

Waahibah: واهبه

Giver; generous.

Waheebah: وهیبه

Giver; generous.

Waheedah: وحیده

Unique; singular; unparalleled; alone.

Wajahat: وجاهت

High position; dignity; comeliness; respect; respectability; appearance.

Wajihah: وجيهه

Of a good appearance; handsome; respectable.

Wakaalat: وكالت

Leadership; advocacy; attorneyship; embassy; agency; commission; proxy.

Wakeelah: وكيله

(Wakilah) The Trustee; the agent.

Waqaar: وقار

Dignity; grace; Name: Waqaarunnisaa

Wardah: ورده

Rose.

Waseefah: وصيفه

Servant; praised.

Waseemah: وسيمه

Of a fine countenance; handsome; comely.

Wazeerah: وزيره

A female minister of state.

Yaameen: يامين

Blessed; auspicious.

Yaar: يار

(Persian) Friend.

Yaaseen: ياسين

Name of a surah in the Holy Quran; A title of The Holy Prophet, Muhammad, peace be upon him.

Yaasir: ياسر

Name of a Sahabi (RA).

Yahya: يحيى

Name of a prophet of Allah Almighty.

Ya'laa: يعلاء

Name of a Sahabi(RA).

Yaqeen: يقين

Belief.

Yaqoot: ياقوت

Ruby; a precious stone; a garnet.

Ya'qoob: يعقوب

Name of a prophet of Allah; father of Hazrat Yousuf(Joseph). Its English Equivalent is Jacob or Israel.

Yasaar: يسار

Name of a Sahabi (RA).

Yathrib: يثرب

(Yasrib): Old name of Madinah Munawwarh before the migration of the Holy Prophet Muhammad peace be upon him.

Yaawar: ياور

(Persian) Aiding; friendly; An assistant; companion; friend.

Yazeed: يزيد

Name of a Sahabi who participated in the battle of Badr.

Yameen: يمين

Right side, blessed.

Yoosuf: يوسف

Name of a prophet of Allah. Its English Equivalent is Joseph.

Younus: يونس

Name of a prophet of Allah. Its English Equivalent is Jonah.

Yusr: يسر

Ease, convenience.

Female Names

Yaaqoot: ياقوت
> Ruby; a precious stone; a garnet.

Yaasmeen: ياسمين
> A sweet-smelling flower called jasmin.

Ya'laa: يعلا
> Name of a Sahabi(RA).

Yumnaa: يُمنى
> Right side; blessed; grace.

Yusairah: يُسيرة
> Name of a Sahabiyyah (RA).

Yusraa: يُسرى
> Left side;easier.

Zaahid: زاهد

Abstinent; one who has no mundane ambitions.

Zaahir: زاهر

A blooming folwer; a bright and shining colour; lofty.

Zaair: زائر

visitor; guest.

Zaakir: ذاكر

(Dhakir) One who constantly praises and remembers Allah Ta'ala..

Zaamin: ضامن

(Daamin) One who stands surety for another; one who helps.

Zaheer: زهير

Blooming; shining; luminous.

Zaid: زيد

Name of a Sahabi who participated in the battle of Badr; He is the only Sahabi who is mentioned in the Holy Quraan by name; and he was one of those Sahabah who were ascribes of the divine revelation.

Zain: زين

Adornment; beauty; grace; honor; to beautify; to decorate. Suitable combination of names: Zainul-Aabideen; Zainud-Deen.

Zaitoon: زيتون

The olive tree or the olive fruit.

Zakaa': ذكاء

(Dhakaa) Keen perception; sharpness of mind; deep insight; sagacity. Name: Zakaa' ud-Deen.

Zakaria : زكريا

(Zakariyyaa)Name of a prophet of Allah; Its English Equivalent is Zacharia.

Zakawaan: ذكوان

(Dhakawaa) Name of a Sahabi who participated in the battle of Badr.

Zaki: ذكى

(Dhaki) One who has a sharp mind and keen perception; intelligent.

Zaki: زكى

Clean, pure.

Zameer: ضمير

(Dameer): Heart; conscience.

Zhaafir: ظافر

(Zaafir): Victorious; conqueror.

Zhaahir: ظاهر

(Zaahir): Apparent; evident ; One of the attributes of Allah Almighty.

Zhafar: ظفر

(Zafar): Victory; triumph; name of a Sahaabi(RA).

Zhafeer: ظفير

(Zafeer): Of firm and resolute intention.

Zhaheer: ظهير

(Zaheer): Assistant; supporter; Name of a Sahabi who participated in the battle of Badr .

Zhareef: ظريف

(Zareef): Polite; witty; good-tempered ingenious; good.

Zhill: ظل

(Zill): Shadow; shade; protection.

Zhuhoor: ظهور

(Zuhoor): Appearing; arising; visibility.

Zia: ضياء

(Diyaa) Light; spender; brilliance.

Zeeshaan: ذيشان

(Dheeshaan) Graceful; distinguished, elegant.

Ziyaad: زياد

Name of a Sahabi who participated in the battle of Badr.

Zubair: زبير

A brave and wise person;Name of a famous Sahabi who was of the 'Ashara-i-Mubashsharah.

Zufar: زفر

Lion; a brave person; an army; a flowing river; ; Name of a great Imaam and jurist.

Zuhaa: ضحى

(Duhaa) Forenoon. Name: Shamsu-Zuhaa.

Zuhair: زهير

Name of a Sahabi who participated in the battle of Badr.

Zulfaqaar: ذوالفقار

(Dhulfaqar) Name of a celebrated sword which fell into the hand of Rasoolullah sallallaahu-alayhi- wasallam in the Battle of Badr and which was presented to Ali(RA). Note: It is incorrect to Say Fiqaar with kasrah).

Zulkifl: ذوالكفل

(Dhulkifl) Name of a prophet of Allah.

Zunnoon: ذوالنون

(Dhunnoon) The title of Hazrat Yoonus (Peace be upon him) meaning The Man of the whale,

Zushshimalain: ذوالشمالين

(Dhushimalin) Name of a Sahabi (RA).

Female Names

Zaahidah: زاهده

Abstinent; lacking mundane ambitions..

Zaaiirah: زائرة

visitor; guest.

Zaakirah: ذاكرة

(Dhaakirah) one who constantly praises and remembers Allah Almighty.

Zaaminah: ضامنه

(Ḍaaminah) One who stands surety for another one who helps.

Zahra': زهرآء

Beautiful; also the name of the lady of jannah, Faatimah(RA).

Zahrah: زهره

The planet Venus; beauty; virtue; elegance; splendor.

Zaib: زيب

(Persian) adornment beauty; elegance.

Zaibaa: زيبا

(Persian) Adorned; beautiful; becoming; befitting; proper; graceful.

Zain: زين

Adornment; beauty; grace;honor; to beautify; to decorate.

Zainab: زينب

Name of the daughter of the Holy Prophet peace be upon him; also the name of Ummul-moomineen, the wife of the Holy Prophet peace be upon him.

Zaitoon: زيتون

The olive tree or the olive fruit.

Zaitoonah: زيتونه

Singular of Zaitoon meaning one olive.

Zakiyyah: ذكيه

(Dhakiyyah) One who has a sharp mind and keen perception; intelligent.

Zameelah: زميله

Friend; colleague.

Zareenah: زرينه

Name of a Sahabiyyah(RA).

Zhaafirah: ظافرة

(Zaafirah) Victorious; conqueror.

Zhaahirah: ظاهرة

(Zaahirah) Apparent; evident; Bright.

Zhafeerah: ظفيره

(Zafeerah): Of firm and resolute intention.

Zhaheerah: ظهيره

(Zaheerah Assistant; supporter.

Zhareefah: ظريفه

(Zareefah) Polite; witty; ingenious; good.

Zinneerah: زنيره
> Name of a Sahabiyyah (RA).

Zarqaa': زرقا
> Blue color.

Zeenat: زينت
> Beauty; elegance; adornment.

Zubaidah: زبيده
> Name of the wife of the Caliph Haroon ur-Rasheed.

Zubdah: زبدة
> Butter.

Zuhairaa': ذهيرا
> Diminutive of Zahraa'. spirit; courage; power; freshness; flower.

Zuhrah: ذهرة
> The planet Venus; beauty; virtue; elegance; splendor.

Zulaikhaa: زليخا
> Name of the famous woman in the days of Hazrat Yousuf (peace be upon him), a prophet of Almighty Allah.

SOME FAMOUS NAMES OF
THE MESSENGERS OF ALLAH:

Ayyoob
DAanyal
Dawood
Ibrahim
Ilyas
Ishaaq
Isma'eel
Looṭ
Moosa
Nooḥ
Sulaiman
'Uzair
Yaḥya
Ya'qoob
Yoonus
Yousuf
Zakaria

THE NAMES OF AL-ASHRAH AL-MUBSHSH-SHARAH:

The names of the ten Sahabah who were given the glad tidinings of their assured attainment of Jannah by the Holy Prophet ﴾ﷺ﴿ are:

(1):Abu Bakr Ṣiddeeque (رضي الله عنه)

(2):'Umar Ibn al-khaṭṭaab(رضي الله عنه)

(3):'Uthmaan Ibn 'Affaan (رضي الله عنه)

(4):Ali Ibn Abi Ṭaalib(رضي الله عنه)

(5):Ṭalhah Ibn 'Ubaidullah(رضي الله عنه);

(6): Zubair Ibn Al-'Awwaam(رضي الله عنه);

(7): Abdur Rahmaan Ibn 'Auf (رضي الله عنه);

(8): Sa'd Ibn Abi Wqqaaṣ(رضي الله عنه);

(9):Sa'eed Ibn Zaid(رضي الله عنه);

(10): Abu 'Ubaidah Ibn Jarrah(رضي الله عنه).

THE NAMES OF THE WIVES OF THE HOLY PROPHET ﷺ:

Khadijah (رضي الله عنها)

Saudah bint Zama'ah (رضي الله عنها)

'A'ishah bint Abi Bakr (رضي الله عنها)

Hafṣah (رضي الله عنها)

Zainab bint Khuzaimah(رضي الله عنها)

Umm Salamah(رضي الله عنها)

Zainab bint jaḥsh(رضي الله عنها)

Juwairyyah(رضي الله عنها)

Umm Ḥabeebah(her name was Ramlah رضي الله عنها)

Ṣafiyyah bint Ḥuyayy (رضي الله عنها)

Maimoonah (رضي الله عنها).

NAMES OF THE CHILDREN OF THE HOLY PROPHET ﷺ:

Ṭaahir(رضي الله عنه).

Ṭayyib (رضي الله عنه).

Ibraaheem (رضي الله عنه).

DAUGHTERS:
   Zainab (رضي الله عنها)
   Faaṭimah (رضي الله عنها)
   Ruqayyah (رضي الله عنها)
   Umm kulthoom (رضي الله عنها)

**THE NAMES OF THE SCRIBES OF THE *WAHI*,
(The Divine Revelation):**
   Khaalid ibn Sa'eed (رضي الله عنه)
   Hanzhalah (رضي الله عنه)
   Yazeed ibn Abi Sufyaan (رضي الله عنه)
   Zaid ibn Thaabit (رضي الله عنه)
   Mu'aawiyah ibn Abi Sufyaan (رضي الله عنه).